**TEACHER'S PET PUBLICATIONS**

PUZZLE PACK
for
The Lion, the Witch and the Wardrobe

based on the book by
C. S. Lewis

Written by
Mary B. Collins

© 2006 Teacher's Pet Publications
All Rights Reserved

The materials in this packet are copyrighted
by Teacher's Pet Publications, Inc.

These pages may be duplicated by the purchaser
for use in the purchaser's own classroom.

Copying any of these materials and distributing them
for any other purpose is a violation of the copyright laws.

© 2006 Teacher's Pet Publications, Inc.
www.tpet.com

INTRODUCTION
If you already own the LitPlan for this title, this Puzzle Pack will refresh your Unit Resource Materials and Vocabulary Resource Materials sections plus give you additional materials you can substitute into the tests.If you do not already have a complete LitPlan, these pages will give you some supplemental materials to use with your own plan. There are two main groups of materials: one set for unit words (such as characters' names, symbols, places, etc.) and one set for vocabulary words associated with the book.

WORD LIST
There is a word list for both the unit words and the vocabulary words. These lists show you which words are being used in the materials and the clues or definitions being used for those words. You may want to give students a word list with clues/definitions to help them, or you may want students to only have a word list (without clues/definitions) if you want them to work a little harder. Both are available for duplication. The word lists can also be your "calling key" for the bingo games.

FILL IN THE BLANK AND MATCHING
There are 4 each of the fill in the blank and matching worksheets for both the unit and vocabulary words. These pages can be used either as extra worksheets for students or as objective parts of a unit test. They can be done individually if students need extra help or as a whole class activity to review the material covered.

MAGIC SQUARES
The magic squares not only reinforce the material covered but also work on reasoning and math skills. Many teachers have told us that their students really enjoy doing these!

WORD SEARCH PUZZLES
The word search words go in all directions, as indicated on your answer keys. Two of the word search puzzles have the clues listed rather than the words. This makes the puzzle a little more difficult, but it reinforces the material better. Two word search puzzles have words only for students who find the clue puzzles too difficult.

CROSSWORD PUZZLES
Both unit and vocabulary word sections have 4 crossword puzzles.

BINGO CARDS
There are 32 individual bingo cards for the unit words and 32 individual bingo cards for the vocabulary words. You can use your word list as a "call list," calling the words at random and marking them off of your list as you go, or you could use the flash cards by cutting them apart and drawing the words at random from a hat (or box or whatever). To make a better review, you might ask for the definition and spelling of each word as you call it out–or you could call out the definitions and have students tell you the words they need to look for on the puzzle.

JUGGLE LETTERS
The vocabulary juggle letter game is intended to help students learn the spellings of the words. One sheet has the definitions listed on it as an extra help for students who need it or to reinforce the definitions if you choose to do so.

FLASH CARDS
We've included a set of vocabulary flash cards you can duplicate, cut, and fold for your students. Some teachers make a few sets for general use by the class; others make a set for each student. Some teachers duplicate them for each student and have the students cut & fold their own. You can cut out just the words and put them in a hat, have each student pick out one word and write the definition and a sentence for that word. Students then swap words and papers, with the next student adding a sentence of his own under the last one. You can have students swap as many times as you like. Each time the student will read the sentences written prior to his own and then add a sentence. You can cut out the words and definitions separately and play "I Have; Who Has?" Each student in the room draws a word and definition. The first student says, "I have (the name of the word). Who has the definition?" The student with the definition reads it then says, "I have (the name of the vocabulary word she has). Who has the definition?" The round continues until all words and definitions have been given.

The Lion, The Witch & The Wardrobe Word List

No.	Word	Clue/Definition
1.	ASLAN	He destroyed winter & killed the Witch.
2.	BATTLE	Aslan and Peter planned this after the White Witch left camp.
3.	BEAVERS	They took the children to Aslan.
4.	BOW	Susan's unused gift: ___ and arrow
5.	CAIR	Castle by the sea; ___ Paravel
6.	CASTLE	It was located between two mountains: Witch's ___
7.	CAVE	Mr. Tumnus's house was a ___.
8.	CENTAUR	Half horse, half man
9.	CHRISTMAS	He gave useful gifts to the children: Father ___
10.	COATS	Children borrowed these from the wardrobe
11.	CORDIAL	Used to save the wounded after the battle
12.	DAGGER	Lucy's gift that she did not use
13.	DWARF	Short servant of the White Witch
14.	EDMUND	___ The Just
15.	FAUN	Mr. Tumnus's race
16.	HORN	Susan used this to call for help.
17.	KNIFE	Witch used it to kill Aslan
18.	LAMP	Lucy met Mr. Tumnus at the ___ post.
19.	LONDON	Home town of the Pevensie children
20.	LUCY	First to enter Narnia
21.	MAUGRIM	Chief of the secret police
22.	MCREADY	She told the children to stay out of trouble.
23.	MICE	They gnawed through Aslan's ropes.
24.	PETER	He killed Maugrim.
25.	PROFESSOR	Owner of the country house where the children stayed
26.	RUMBLEBUFFIN	A friendly giant
27.	SARDINES	Tea-time treat
28.	SHIELD	It contained a red lion crest.
29.	SLEDGE	White Witch's transportation
30.	SNOW	Nature's white winter covering
31.	SPRING	It arrived with Aslan.
32.	STAG	Hunted by the adult Pevensies; White ___
33.	STATUES	Aslan's breath freed these.
34.	STONE	Place of sacrifice; ___ Table
35.	SUSAN	She carried a horn.
36.	SWORD	Used to kill Maugrim
37.	TUMNUS	The Faun who had tea with Lucy
38.	TURKISH	Edmund's temptation: ___ Delight
39.	WAND	Edmund broke the White Witch's
40.	WARDROBE	Doorway to Narnia
41.	WITCH	She was half Jinn & half giantess; White ___
42.	WOLF	Sir Peter ____'s Bane
43.	WOLVES	Attacked Susan and Lucy

The Lion, The Witch & The Wardrobe Fill In The Blank 1

_____ 1. He destroyed winter & killed the Witch.

_____ 2. The Faun who had tea with Lucy

_____ 3. Place of sacrifice; ___ Table

_____ 4. Edmund's temptation: ___ Delight

_____ 5. Attacked Susan and Lucy

_____ 6. Doorway to Narnia

_____ 7. Tea-time treat

_____ 8. Used to save the wounded after the battle

_____ 9. Chief of the secret police

_____ 10. Castle by the sea; ___ Paravel

_____ 11. ___ The Just

_____ 12. She carried a horn.

_____ 13. Short servant of the White Witch

_____ 14. Witch used it to kill Aslan

_____ 15. First to enter Narnia

_____ 16. They gnawed through Aslan's ropes.

_____ 17. She told the children to stay out of trouble.

_____ 18. White Witch's transportation

_____ 19. Aslan's breath freed these.

_____ 20. Mr. Tumnus's race

The Lion, The Witch & The Wardrobe Fill In The Blank 1 Answer Key

ASLAN	1. He destroyed winter & killed the Witch.
TUMNUS	2. The Faun who had tea with Lucy
STONE	3. Place of sacrifice; ___ Table
TURKISH	4. Edmund's temptation: ___ Delight
WOLVES	5. Attacked Susan and Lucy
WARDROBE	6. Doorway to Narnia
SARDINES	7. Tea-time treat
CORDIAL	8. Used to save the wounded after the battle
MAUGRIM	9. Chief of the secret police
CAIR	10. Castle by the sea; ___ Paravel
EDMUND	11. ___ The Just
SUSAN	12. She carried a horn.
DWARF	13. Short servant of the White Witch
KNIFE	14. Witch used it to kill Aslan
LUCY	15. First to enter Narnia
MICE	16. They gnawed through Aslan's ropes.
MCREADY	17. She told the children to stay out of trouble.
SLEDGE	18. White Witch's transportation
STATUES	19. Aslan's breath freed these.
FAUN	20. Mr. Tumnus's race

The Lion, The Witch & The Wardrobe Fill In The Blank 2

_____ 1. Lucy's gift that she did not use

_____ 2. It arrived with Aslan.

_____ 3. Aslan and Peter planned this after the White Witch left camp.

_____ 4. Tea-time treat

_____ 5. Mr. Tumnus's house was a ___.

_____ 6. Doorway to Narnia

_____ 7. He destroyed winter & killed the Witch.

_____ 8. They gnawed through Aslan's ropes.

_____ 9. Susan's unused gift: ___ and arrow

_____ 10. Lucy met Mr. Tumnus at the ___ post.

_____ 11. Used to kill Maugrim

_____ 12. She was half Jinn & half giantess; White ___

_____ 13. They took the children to Aslan.

_____ 14. Place of sacrifice; ___ Table

_____ 15. First to enter Narnia

_____ 16. Edmund broke the White Witch's

_____ 17. It was located between two mountains: Witch's ___

_____ 18. Half horse, half man

_____ 19. She told the children to stay out of trouble.

_____ 20. Children borrowed these from the wardrobe

The Lion, The Witch & The Wardrobe Fill In The Blank 2 Answer Key

DAGGER	1. Lucy's gift that she did not use
SPRING	2. It arrived with Aslan.
BATTLE	3. Aslan and Peter planned this after the White Witch left camp.
SARDINES	4. Tea-time treat
CAVE	5. Mr. Tumnus's house was a ___.
WARDROBE	6. Doorway to Narnia
ASLAN	7. He destroyed winter & killed the Witch.
MICE	8. They gnawed through Aslan's ropes.
BOW	9. Susan's unused gift: ___ and arrow
LAMP	10. Lucy met Mr. Tumnus at the ___ post.
SWORD	11. Used to kill Maugrim
WITCH	12. She was half Jinn & half giantess; White ___
BEAVERS	13. They took the children to Aslan.
STONE	14. Place of sacrifice; ___ Table
LUCY	15. First to enter Narnia
WAND	16. Edmund broke the White Witch's
CASTLE	17. It was located between two mountains: Witch's ___
CENTAUR	18. Half horse, half man
MCREADY	19. She told the children to stay out of trouble.
COATS	20. Children borrowed these from the wardrobe

The Lion, The Witch & The Wardrobe Fill In The Blank 3

_____ 1. A friendly giant

_____ 2. Edmund's temptation: ___ Delight

_____ 3. The Faun who had tea with Lucy

_____ 4. Half horse, half man

_____ 5. Lucy's gift that she did not use

_____ 6. Used to kill Maugrim

_____ 7. First to enter Narnia

_____ 8. Castle by the sea; ___ Paravel

_____ 9. It was located between two mountains: Witch's ___

_____ 10. It arrived with Aslan.

_____ 11. He killed Maugrim.

_____ 12. She was half Jinn & half giantess; White ___

_____ 13. Chief of the secret police

_____ 14. He destroyed winter & killed the Witch.

_____ 15. Aslan's breath freed these.

_____ 16. Hunted by the adult Pevensies; White ___

_____ 17. Witch used it to kill Asaln

_____ 18. Susan's unused gift: ___ and arrow

_____ 19. Aslan and Peter planned this after the White Witch left camp.

_____ 20. Nature's white winter covering

The Lion, The Witch & The Wardrobe Fill In The Blank 3 Answer Key

RUMBLEBUFFIN	1. A friendly giant
TURKISH	2. Edmund's temptation: ___ Delight
TUMNUS	3. The Faun who had tea with Lucy
CENTAUR	4. Half horse, half man
DAGGER	5. Lucy's gift that she did not use
SWORD	6. Used to kill Maugrim
LUCY	7. First to enter Narnia
CAIR	8. Castle by the sea; ___ Paravel
CASTLE	9. It was located between two mountains: Witch's ___
SPRING	10. It arrived with Aslan.
PETER	11. He killed Maugrim.
WITCH	12. She was half Jinn & half giantess; White ___
MAUGRIM	13. Chief of the secret police
ASLAN	14. He destroyed winter & killed the Witch.
STATUES	15. Aslan's breath freed these.
STAG	16. Hunted by the adult Pevensies; White ___
KNIFE	17. Witch used it to kill Aslan
BOW	18. Susan's unused gift: ___ and arrow
BATTLE	19. Aslan and Peter planned this after the White Witch left camp.
SNOW	20. Nature's white winter covering

The Lion, The Witch & The Wardrobe Fill In The Blank 4

1. They gnawed through Aslan's ropes.
2. Aslan and Peter planned this after the White Witch left camp.
3. Aslan's breath freed these.
4. ___ The Just
5. Owner of the country house where the children stayed
6. Susan's unused gift: ___ and arrow
7. Lucy's gift that she did not use
8. Edmund broke the White Witch's
9. Half horse, half man
10. Short servant of the White Witch
11. First to enter Narnia
12. Doorway to Narnia
13. Castle by the sea; ___ Paravel
14. A friendly giant
15. Chief of the secret police
16. Witch used it to kill Aslan
17. Nature's white winter covering
18. Mr. Tumnus's race
19. Lucy met Mr. Tumnus at the ___ post.
20. Edmund's temptation: ___ Delight

The Lion, The Witch & The Wardrobe Fill In The Blank 4 Answer Key

MICE	1. They gnawed through Aslan's ropes.
BATTLE	2. Aslan and Peter planned this after the White Witch left camp.
STATUES	3. Aslan's breath freed these.
EDMUND	4. ___ The Just
PROFESSOR	5. Owner of the country house where the children stayed
BOW	6. Susan's unused gift: ___ and arrow
DAGGER	7. Lucy's gift that she did not use
WAND	8. Edmund broke the White Witch's
CENTAUR	9. Half horse, half man
DWARF	10. Short servant of the White Witch
LUCY	11. First to enter Narnia
WARDROBE	12. Doorway to Narnia
CAIR	13. Castle by the sea; ___ Paravel
RUMBLEBUFFIN	14. A friendly giant
MAUGRIM	15. Chief of the secret police
KNIFE	16. Witch used it to kill Aslan
SNOW	17. Nature's white winter covering
FAUN	18. Mr. Tumnus's race
LAMP	19. Lucy met Mr. Tumnus at the ___ post.
TURKISH	20. Edmund's temptation: ___ Delight

The Lion, The Witch & The Wardrobe Matching 1

___ 1. LUCY   A. They took the children to Aslan.
___ 2. WOLVES   B. Edmund broke the White Witch's
___ 3. CAVE   C. Owner of the country house where the children stayed
___ 4. CHRISTMAS   D. Witch used it to kill Aslan
___ 5. STATUES   E. Lucy met Mr. Tumnus at the ___ post.
___ 6. SHIELD   F. The Faun who had tea with Lucy
___ 7. WOLF   G. Castle by the sea; ___ Paravel
___ 8. CENTAUR   H. He gave useful gifts to the children: Father ___
___ 9. WAND   I. Hunted by the adult Pevensies; White ___
___10. PETER   J. Attacked Susan and Lucy
___11. TUMNUS   K. Aslan and Peter planned this after the White Witch left camp.
___12. CAIR   L. First to enter Narnia
___13. MICE   M. He killed Maugrim.
___14. ASLAN   N. It contained a red lion crest.
___15. DAGGER   O. ___ The Just
___16. SLEDGE   P. It was located between two mountains: Witch's ___
___17. BATTLE   Q. White Witch's transportation
___18. STAG   R. Aslan's breath freed these.
___19. CASTLE   S. He destroyed winter & killed the Witch.
___20. KNIFE   T. Sir Peter ____'s Bane
___21. BEAVERS   U. Tea-time treat
___22. EDMUND   V. Lucy's gift that she did not use
___23. SARDINES   W. Half horse, half man
___24. PROFESSOR   X. They gnawed through Alan's ropes.
___25. LAMP   Y. Mr. Tumnus's house was a ___.

The Lion, The Witch & The Wardrobe Matching 1 Answer Key

L - 1. LUCY	A. They took the children to Aslan.
J - 2. WOLVES	B. Edmund broke the White Witch's
Y - 3. CAVE	C. Owner of the country house where the children stayed
H - 4. CHRISTMAS	D. Witch used it to kill Aslan
R - 5. STATUES	E. Lucy met Mr. Tumnus at the ___ post.
N - 6. SHIELD	F. The Faun who had tea with Lucy
T - 7. WOLF	G. Castle by the sea; ___ Paravel
W - 8. CENTAUR	H. He gave useful gifts to the children: Father ___
B - 9. WAND	I. Hunted by the adult Pevensies; White ___
M -10. PETER	J. Attacked Susan and Lucy
F -11. TUMNUS	K. Aslan and Peter planned this after the White Witch left camp.
G -12. CAIR	L. First to enter Narnia
X -13. MICE	M. He killed Maugrim.
S -14. ASLAN	N. It contained a red lion crest.
V -15. DAGGER	O. ___ The Just
Q -16. SLEDGE	P. It was located between two mountains: Witch's ___
K -17. BATTLE	Q. White Witch's transportation
I -18. STAG	R. Aslan's breath freed these.
P -19. CASTLE	S. He destroyed winter & killed the Witch.
D -20. KNIFE	T. Sir Peter ____'s Bane
A -21. BEAVERS	U. Tea-time treat
O -22. EDMUND	V. Lucy's gift that she did not use
U -23. SARDINES	W. Half horse, half man
C -24. PROFESSOR	X. They gnawed through Aslan's ropes.
E -25. LAMP	Y. Mr. Tumnus's house was a ___.

Copyrighted

The Lion, The Witch & The Wardrobe Matching 2

___ 1. SUSAN
___ 2. BATTLE
___ 3. TUMNUS
___ 4. CASTLE
___ 5. CAVE
___ 6. SARDINES
___ 7. EDMUND
___ 8. TURKISH
___ 9. LUCY
___ 10. DWARF
___ 11. WAND
___ 12. WITCH
___ 13. MCREADY
___ 14. STATUES
___ 15. RUMBLEBUFFIN
___ 16. ASLAN
___ 17. CAIR
___ 18. CHRISTMAS
___ 19. COATS
___ 20. BOW
___ 21. PETER
___ 22. FAUN
___ 23. SHIELD
___ 24. WOLVES
___ 25. LAMP

A. Mr. Tumnus's house was a ___.
B. First to enter Narnia
C. A friendly giant
D. It was located between two mountains: Witch's ___
E. ___ The Just
F. She was half Jinn & half giantess; White ___
G. Children borrowed these from the wardrobe
H. Aslan and Peter planned this after the White Witch left camp.
I. He gave useful gifts to the children: Father ___
J. He destroyed winter & killed the Witch.
K. Edmund's temptation: ___ Delight
L. It contained a red lion crest.
M. Lucy met Mr. Tumnus at the ___ post.
N. Attacked Susan and Lucy
O. He killed Maugrim.
P. Susan's unused gift: ___ and arrow
Q. Short servant of the White Witch
R. Edmund broke the White Witch's
S. The Faun who had tea with Lucy
T. Aslan's breath freed these.
U. She carried a horn.
V. Mr. Tumnus's race
W. She told the children to stay out of trouble.
X. Tea-time treat
Y. Castle by the sea; ___ Paravel

The Lion, The Witch & The Wardrobe Matching 2 Answer Key

U - 1. SUSAN   A. Mr. Tumnus's house was a ___.
H - 2. BATTLE   B. First to enter Narnia
S - 3. TUMNUS   C. A friendly giant
D - 4. CASTLE   D. It was located between two mountains: Witch's ___
A - 5. CAVE   E. ___ The Just
X - 6. SARDINES   F. She was half Jinn & half giantess; White ___
E - 7. EDMUND   G. Children borrowed these from the wardrobe
K - 8. TURKISH   H. Aslan and Peter planned this after the White Witch left camp.
B - 9. LUCY   I. He gave useful gifts to the children: Father ___
Q -10. DWARF   J. He destroyed winter & killed the Witch.
R -11. WAND   K. Edmund's temptation: ___ Delight
F -12. WITCH   L. It contained a red lion crest.
W -13. MCREADY   M. Lucy met Mr. Tumnus at the ___ post.
T -14. STATUES   N. Attacked Susan and Lucy
C -15. RUMBLEBUFFIN   O. He killed Maugrim.
J -16. ASLAN   P. Susan's unused gift: ___ and arrow
Y -17. CAIR   Q. Short servant of the White Witch
I -18. CHRISTMAS   R. Edmund broke the White Witch's
G -19. COATS   S. The Faun who had tea with Lucy
P -20. BOW   T. Aslan's breath freed these.
O -21. PETER   U. She carried a horn.
V -22. FAUN   V. Mr. Tumnus's race
L -23. SHIELD   W. She told the children to stay out of trouble.
N -24. WOLVES   X. Tea-time treat
M -25. LAMP   Y. Castle by the sea; ___ Paravel

The Lion, The Witch & The Wardrobe Matching 3

___ 1. PROFESSOR   A. Children borrowed these from the wardrobe
___ 2. CASTLE   B. She told the children to stay out of trouble.
___ 3. COATS   C. She carried a horn.
___ 4. SWORD   D. Lucy's gift that she did not use
___ 5. WAND   E. She was half Jinn & half giantess; White ___
___ 6. WARDROBE   F. Edmund broke the White Witch's
___ 7. MICE   G. He killed Maugrim.
___ 8. MCREADY   H. A friendly giant
___ 9. LONDON   I. It was located between two mountains: Witch's ___
___10. WOLF   J. Sir Peter ____'s Bane
___11. LAMP   K. Place of sacrifice; ___ Table
___12. STATUES   L. They gnawed through Alan's ropes.
___13. STAG   M. White Witch's transportation
___14. TUMNUS   N. Attacked Susan and Lucy
___15. BEAVERS   O. Lucy met Mr. Tumnus at the ___ post.
___16. MAUGRIM   P. It contained a red lion crest.
___17. WOLVES   Q. Aslan's breath freed these.
___18. SHIELD   R. Used to kill Maugrim
___19. DAGGER   S. Home town of the Pevensie children
___20. WITCH   T. Owner of the country house where the children stayed
___21. PETER   U. Hunted by the adult Pevensies; White ___
___22. RUMBLEBUFFIN   V. The Faun who had tea with Lucy
___23. SLEDGE   W. Doorway to Narnia
___24. SUSAN   X. Chief of the secret police
___25. STONE   Y. They took the children to Aslan.

The Lion, The Witch & The Wardrobe Matching 3 Answer Key

T - 1. PROFESSOR	A.	Children borrowed these from the wardrobe
I - 2. CASTLE	B.	She told the children to stay out of trouble.
A - 3. COATS	C.	She carried a horn.
R - 4. SWORD	D.	Lucy's gift that she did not use
F - 5. WAND	E.	She was half Jinn & half giantess; White ___
W - 6. WARDROBE	F.	Edmund broke the White Witch's
L - 7. MICE	G.	He killed Maugrim.
B - 8. MCREADY	H.	A friendly giant
S - 9. LONDON	I.	It was located between two mountains: Witch's ___
J - 10. WOLF	J.	Sir Peter ____'s Bane
O - 11. LAMP	K.	Place of sacrifice; ___ Table
Q - 12. STATUES	L.	They gnawed through Alan's ropes.
U - 13. STAG	M.	White Witch's transportation
V - 14. TUMNUS	N.	Attacked Susan and Lucy
Y - 15. BEAVERS	O.	Lucy met Mr. Tumnus at the ___ post.
X - 16. MAUGRIM	P.	It contained a red lion crest.
N - 17. WOLVES	Q.	Aslan's breath freed these.
P - 18. SHIELD	R.	Used to kill Maugrim
D - 19. DAGGER	S.	Home town of the Pevensie children
E - 20. WITCH	T.	Owner of the country house where the children stayed
G - 21. PETER	U.	Hunted by the adult Pevensies; White ___
H - 22. RUMBLEBUFFIN	V.	The Faun who had tea with Lucy
M - 23. SLEDGE	W.	Doorway to Narnia
C - 24. SUSAN	X.	Chief of the secret police
K - 25. STONE	Y.	They took the children to Aslan.

The Lion, The Witch & The Wardrobe Matching 4

___ 1. EDMUND   A. Mr. Tumnus's race
___ 2. SLEDGE   B. Susan used this to call for help.
___ 3. KNIFE   C. Witch used it to kill Aslan
___ 4. WAND   D. Owner of the country house where the children stayed
___ 5. WOLVES   E. First to enter Narnia
___ 6. CENTAUR   F. Used to kill Maugrim
___ 7. SPRING   G. It arrived with Aslan.
___ 8. STONE   H. She carried a horn.
___ 9. MCREADY   I. Susan's unused gift: ___ and arrow
___10. BATTLE   J. ___ The Just
___11. STATUES   K. It was located between two mountains: Witch's ___
___12. CASTLE   L. Place of sacrifice; ___ Table
___13. PROFESSOR   M. Aslan's breath freed these.
___14. ASLAN   N. Tea-time treat
___15. HORN   O. Mr. Tumnus's house was a ___.
___16. SUSAN   P. Edmund broke the White Witch's
___17. CAVE   Q. Used to save the wounded after the battle
___18. TUMNUS   R. Attacked Susan and Lucy
___19. FAUN   S. He destroyed winter & killed the Witch.
___20. CORDIAL   T. White Witch's transportation
___21. SARDINES   U. The Faun who had tea with Lucy
___22. CAIR   V. Castle by the sea; ___ Paravel
___23. SWORD   W. Half horse, half man
___24. BOW   X. She told the children to stay out of trouble.
___25. LUCY   Y. Aslan and Peter planned this after the White Witch left camp.

The Lion, The Witch & The Wardrobe Matching 4 Answer Key

J - 1.	EDMUND	A.	Mr. Tumnus's race
T - 2.	SLEDGE	B.	Susan used this to call for help.
C - 3.	KNIFE	C.	Witch used it to kill Aslan
P - 4.	WAND	D.	Owner of the country house where the children stayed
R - 5.	WOLVES	E.	First to enter Narnia
W - 6.	CENTAUR	F.	Used to kill Maugrim
G - 7.	SPRING	G.	It arrived with Aslan.
L - 8.	STONE	H.	She carried a horn.
X - 9.	MCREADY	I.	Susan's unused gift: ___ and arrow
Y - 10.	BATTLE	J.	___ The Just
M - 11.	STATUES	K.	It was located between two mountains: Witch's ___
K - 12.	CASTLE	L.	Place of sacrifice; ___ Table
D - 13.	PROFESSOR	M.	Aslan's breath freed these.
S - 14.	ASLAN	N.	Tea-time treat
B - 15.	HORN	O.	Mr. Tumnus's house was a ___.
H - 16.	SUSAN	P.	Edmund broke the White Witch's
O - 17.	CAVE	Q.	Used to save the wounded after the battle
U - 18.	TUMNUS	R.	Attacked Susan and Lucy
A - 19.	FAUN	S.	He destroyed winter & killed the Witch.
Q - 20.	CORDIAL	T.	White Witch's transportation
N - 21.	SARDINES	U.	The Faun who had tea with Lucy
V - 22.	CAIR	V.	Castle by the sea; ___ Paravel
F - 23.	SWORD	W.	Half horse, half man
I - 24.	BOW	X.	She told the children to stay out of trouble.
E - 25.	LUCY	Y.	Aslan and Peter planned this after the White Witch left camp.

The Lion, The Witch & The Wardrobe Magic Squares 1

Match the definition with the vocabulary word. Put your answers in the magic squares below. When your answers are correct, all columns and rows will add to the same number.

A. WOLF
B. LONDON
C. STONE
D. BATTLE
E. MCREADY
F. SPRING
G. SUSAN
H. EDMUND
I. HORN
J. MICE
K. ASLAN
L. LAMP
M. MAUGRIM
N. DWARF
O. SWORD
P. CENTAUR

1. Home town of the Pevensie children
2. She carried a horn.
3. He destroyed winter & killed the Witch.
4. Short servant of the White Witch
5. Chief of the secret police
6. Lucy met Mr. Tumnus at the ___ post.
7. ___ The Just
8. Sir Peter ____'s Bane
9. Half horse, half man
10. Susan used this to call for help.
11. She told the children to stay out of trouble.
12. Aslan and Peter planned this after the White Witch left camp.
13. Place of sacrifice; ___ Table
14. It arrived with Aslan.
15. They gnawed through Aslan's ropes.
16. Used to kill Maugrim

A=	B=	C=	D=
E=	F=	G=	H=
I=	J=	K=	L=
M=	N=	O=	P=

The Lion, The Witch & The Wardrobe Magic Squares 1 Answer Key

Match the definition with the vocabulary word. Put your answers in the magic squares below. When your answers are correct, all columns and rows will add to the same number.

A. WOLF
B. LONDON
C. STONE
D. BATTLE
E. MCREADY
F. SPRING
G. SUSAN
H. EDMUND
I. HORN
J. MICE
K. ASLAN
L. LAMP
M. MAUGRIM
N. DWARF
O. SWORD
P. CENTAUR

1. Home town of the Pevensie children
2. She carried a horn.
3. He destroyed winter & killed the Witch.
4. Short servant of the White Witch
5. Chief of the secret police
6. Lucy met Mr. Tumnus at the ___ post.
7. ___ The Just
8. Sir Peter ____'s Bane
9. Half horse, half man
10. Susan used this to call for help.
11. She told the children to stay out of trouble.
12. Aslan and Peter planned this after the White Witch left camp.
13. Place of sacrifice; ___ Table
14. It arrived with Aslan.
15. They gnawed through Aslan's ropes.
16. Used to kill Maugrim

A=8	B=1	C=13	D=12
E=11	F=14	G=2	H=7
I=10	J=15	K=3	L=6
M=5	N=4	O=16	P=9

The Lion, The Witch & The Wardrobe Magic Squares 2

Match the definition with the vocabulary word. Put your answers in the magic squares below. When your answers are correct, all columns and rows will add to the same number.

A. MICE
B. CHRISTMAS
C. LUCY
D. MCREADY
E. STAG
F. COATS
G. RUMBLEBUFFIN
H. WAND
I. CORDIAL
J. SPRING
K. KNIFE
L. CASTLE
M. STATUES
N. DAGGER
O. BOW
P. PETER

1. Aslan's breath freed these.
2. Children borrowed these from the wardrobe
3. Edmund broke the White Witch's
4. Susan's unused gift: ___ and arrow
5. It was located between two mountains: Witch's ___
6. First to enter Narnia
7. They gnawed through Alan's ropes.
8. It arrived with Aslan.
9. Witch used it to kill Aslan
10. She told the children to stay out of trouble.
11. He gave useful gifts to the children: Father ___
12. Used to save the wounded after the battle
13. Lucy's gift that she did not use
14. Hunted by the adult Pevensies; White ___
15. A friendly giant
16. He killed Maugrim.

A=	B=	C=	D=
E=	F=	G=	H=
I=	J=	K=	L=
M=	N=	O=	P=

The Lion, The Witch & The Wardrobe Magic Squares 2 Answer Key

Match the definition with the vocabulary word. Put your answers in the magic squares below. When your answers are correct, all columns and rows will add to the same number.

A. MICE
B. CHRISTMAS
C. LUCY
D. MCREADY
E. STAG
F. COATS
G. RUMBLEBUFFIN
H. WAND
I. CORDIAL
J. SPRING
K. KNIFE
L. CASTLE
M. STATUES
N. DAGGER
O. BOW
P. PETER

1. Aslan's breath freed these.
2. Children borrowed these from the wardrobe
3. Edmund broke the White Witch's
4. Susan's unused gift: ___ and arrow
5. It was located between two mountains: Witch's ___
6. First to enter Narnia
7. They gnawed through Alan's ropes.
8. It arrived with Aslan.
9. Witch used it to kill Aslan
10. She told the children to stay out of trouble.
11. He gave useful gifts to the children: Father ___
12. Used to save the wounded after the battle
13. Lucy's gift that she did not use
14. Hunted by the adult Pevensies; White ___
15. A friendly giant
16. He killed Maugrim.

A=7	B=11	C=6	D=10
E=14	F=2	G=15	H=3
I=12	J=8	K=9	L=5
M=1	N=13	O=4	P=16

The Lion, The Witch & The Wardrobe Magic Squares 3

Match the definition with the vocabulary word. Put your answers in the magic squares below. When your answers are correct, all columns and rows will add to the same number.

A. MCREADY
B. FAUN
C. LONDON
D. STATUES
E. SWORD
F. CASTLE
G. EDMUND
H. SHIELD
I. WAND
J. SARDINES
K. SLEDGE
L. HORN
M. ASLAN
N. KNIFE
O. BATTLE
P. MAUGRIM

1. Aslan and Peter planned this after the White Witch left camp.
2. Aslan's breath freed these.
3. Tea-time treat
4. Used to kill Maugrim
5. Edmund broke the White Witch's
6. It was located between two mountains: Witch's ___
7. Chief of the secret police
8. Home town of the Pevensie children
9. It contained a red lion crest.
10. White Witch's transportation
11. She told the children to stay out of trouble.
12. Witch used it to kill Aslan
13. Mr. Tumnus's race
14. He destroyed winter & killed the Witch.
15. ___ The Just
16. Susan used this to call for help.

A=	B=	C=	D=
E=	F=	G=	H=
I=	J=	K=	L=
M=	N=	O=	P=

The Lion, The Witch & The Wardrobe Magic Squares 3 Answer Key

Match the definition with the vocabulary word. Put your answers in the magic squares below. When your answers are correct, all columns and rows will add to the same number.

A. MCREADY
B. FAUN
C. LONDON
D. STATUES
E. SWORD
F. CASTLE
G. EDMUND
H. SHIELD
I. WAND
J. SARDINES
K. SLEDGE
L. HORN
M. ASLAN
N. KNIFE
O. BATTLE
P. MAUGRIM

1. Aslan and Peter planned this after the White Witch left camp.
2. Aslan's breath freed these.
3. Tea-time treat
4. Used to kill Maugrim
5. Edmund broke the White Witch's
6. It was located between two mountains: Witch's ___
7. Chief of the secret police
8. Home town of the Pevensie children
9. It contained a red lion crest.
10. White Witch's transportation
11. She told the children to stay out of trouble.
12. Witch used it to kill Aslan
13. Mr. Tumnus's race
14. He destroyed winter & killed the Witch.
15. ___ The Just
16. Susan used this to call for help.

A=11	B=13	C=8	D=2
E=4	F=6	G=15	H=9
I=5	J=3	K=10	L=16
M=14	N=12	O=1	P=7

The Lion, The Witch & The Wardrobe Magic Squares 4

Match the definition with the vocabulary word. Put your answers in the magic squares below. When your answers are correct, all columns and rows will add to the same number.

A. COATS
B. SPRING
C. WARDROBE
D. STONE
E. LONDON
F. MCREADY
G. SHIELD
H. CAIR
I. EDMUND
J. PETER
K. MAUGRIM
L. DAGGER
M. WOLVES
N. LAMP
O. ASLAN
P. STAG

1. Children borrowed these from the wardrobe
2. Lucy met Mr. Tumnus at the ___ post.
3. He killed Maugrim.
4. Home town of the Pevensie children
5. It contained a red lion crest.
6. Lucy's gift that she did not use
7. Hunted by the adult Pevensies; White ___
8. Doorway to Narnia
9. He destroyed winter & killed the Witch.
10. Place of sacrifice; ___ Table
11. Castle by the sea; ___ Paravel
12. Chief of the secret police
13. ___ The Just
14. She told the children to stay out of trouble.
15. It arrived with Aslan.
16. Attacked Susan and Lucy

A=	B=	C=	D=
E=	F=	G=	H=
I=	J=	K=	L=
M=	N=	O=	P=

The Lion, The Witch & The Wardrobe Magic Squares 4 Answer Key

Match the definition with the vocabulary word. Put your answers in the magic squares below. When your answers are correct, all columns and rows will add to the same number.

A. COATS
B. SPRING
C. WARDROBE
D. STONE
E. LONDON
F. MCREADY
G. SHIELD
H. CAIR
I. EDMUND
J. PETER
K. MAUGRIM
L. DAGGER
M. WOLVES
N. LAMP
O. ASLAN
P. STAG

1. Children borrowed these from the wardrobe
2. Lucy met Mr. Tumnus at the ___ post.
3. He killed Maugrim.
4. Home town of the Pevensie children
5. It contained a red lion crest.
6. Lucy's gift that she did not use
7. Hunted by the adult Pevensies; White ___
8. Doorway to Narnia
9. He destroyed winter & killed the Witch.
10. Place of sacrifice; ___ Table
11. Castle by the sea; ___ Paravel
12. Chief of the secret police
13. ___ The Just
14. She told the children to stay out of trouble.
15. It arrived with Aslan.
16. Attacked Susan and Lucy

A=1	B=15	C=8	D=10
E=4	F=14	G=5	H=11
I=13	J=3	K=12	L=6
M=16	N=2	O=9	P=7

The Lion, The Witch & The Wardrobe Word Search 1

```
S W O R D C O R D I A L W I T C H M B Q
P A H W Z A Y Z J W N D R M J H V C A Q
R L R F D C S H C H A X M B J R L R T Y
O X L D J L E L W E T R E P T I B E T S
F N O H I V Z C A U N A F Z R S B A L M
E I N M A N W S R N V T W I U T X D E N
S F D C M D E K D E P B A S N M H Y Y S
S F O S R I S R Y Y C A U S A L C P J
O U N E H S Q S O M N N S U R S U Y S K
R B T U H D F Y B P F P N H Y L R Y G Z
L E J T S V Q Z E M W M Y F I X X S R Y
P L T A T M H P X D U H W A H E T L G H
N B K T C W H K M T G N S U D N L E E V
G M X S V O Q V C N Z M K N I F E D D K
S U Z B C L D S I C X P A Q O C Z G M R
F R Q O X V M R W H M W Z D I W S E U Q
J T A M K E P W O A O V Y M N T Q D N M
S T O N E S N S L M I R G U A M F L D C
S D A G G E R T F B O W N G C A S T L E
```

A friendly giant (12)
Aslan and Peter planned this after the White Witch left camp. (6)
Aslan's breath freed these. (7)
Attacked Susan and Lucy (6)
Castle by the sea; ___ Paravel (4)
Chief of the secret police (7)
Children borrowed these from the wardrobe (5)
Doorway to Narnia (8)
Edmund broke the White Witch's (4)
Edmund's temptation: ___ Delight (7)
First to enter Narnia (4)
Half horse, half man (7)
He destroyed winter & killed the Witch. (5)
He gave useful gifts to the children: Father ___ (9)
He killed Maugrim. (5)
Home town of the Pevensie children (6)
Hunted by the adult Pevensies; White ___ (4)
It arrived with Aslan. (6)
It contained a red lion crest. (6)
It was located between two mountains: Witch's ___ (6)
Lucy met Mr. Tumnus at the ___ post. (4)
Lucy's gift that she did not use (6)
Mr. Tumnus's house was a ___. (4)
Mr. Tumnus's race (4)
Nature's white winter covering (4)
Owner of the country house where the children stayed (9)
Place of sacrifice; ___ Table (5)
She carried a horn. (5)
She told the children to stay out of trouble. (7)
She was half Jinn & half giantess; White ___ (5)
Short servant of the White Witch (5)
Sir Peter ____'s Bane (4)
Susan used this to call for help. (4)
Susan's unused gift: ___ and arrow (3)
Tea-time treat (8)
The Faun who had tea with Lucy (6)
They gnawed through Aslan's ropes. (4)
They took the children to Aslan. (7)
Used to kill Maugrim (5)
Used to save the wounded after the battle (7)
White Witch's transportation (6)
Witch used it to kill Aslan (5)
___ The Just (6)

The Lion, The Witch & The Wardrobe Word Search 1 Answer Key

```
S W O R D C O R D I A L W I T C H M B
P A        A       W              H  C A
R R        S    C    A      B     R  R T
O L  D     E L W E T R E          I  E T
F N  O  I V   A U N A F     R S   A  A L
E I  N  A N   R N V T       I U   T  D E
S F  D C   E K D E          A S M Y  Y
S F  O S R   I S R        C A U S A  C
O U  N E S   S S O        N S U R S  U
R B  T U H       B        N H   L
  E    T         E      M   F I    S
P L    A       U            A   E  L
  B    T   W     T G   S U  D   L  E E
  M    S   O       N   K N  I F E  D D
  U      C L           P A  O C    G M
  R      O V   R W H M W    I W S  E U
        A    E P O A O        M T    N
S T O N E S    L M I R G U A M       D
S D A G G E R  F B O W N G C A S T L E
```

A friendly giant (12)
Aslan and Peter planned this after the White Witch left camp. (6)
Aslan's breath freed these. (7)
Attacked Susan and Lucy (6)
Castle by the sea; ___ Paravel (4)
Chief of the secret police (7)
Children borrowed these from the wardrobe (5)
Doorway to Narnia (8)
Edmund broke the White Witch's (4)
Edmund's temptation: ___ Delight (7)
First to enter Narnia (4)
Half horse, half man (7)
He destroyed winter & killed the Witch. (5)
He gave useful gifts to the children: Father ___ (9)
He killed Maugrim. (5)
Home town of the Pevensie children (6)
Hunted by the adult Pevensies; White ___ (4)
It arrived with Aslan. (6)
It contained a red lion crest. (6)
It was located between two mountains: Witch's ___ (6)
Lucy met Mr. Tumnus at the ___ post. (4)

Lucy's gift that she did not use (6)
Mr. Tumnus's house was a ___. (4)
Mr. Tumnus's race (4)
Nature's white winter covering (4)
Owner of the country house where the children stayed (9)
Place of sacrifice; ___ Table (5)
She carried a horn. (5)
She told the children to stay out of trouble. (7)
She was half Jinn & half giantess; White ___ (5)
Short servant of the White Witch (5)
Sir Peter ____'s Bane (4)
Susan used this to call for help. (4)
Susan's unused gift: ___ and arrow (3)
Tea-time treat (8)
The Faun who had tea with Lucy (6)
They gnawed through Aslan's ropes. (4)
They took the children to Aslan. (7)
Used to kill Maugrim (5)
Used to save the wounded after the battle (7)
White Witch's transportation (6)
Witch used it to kill Aslan (5)
___ The Just (6)

The Lion, The Witch & The Wardrobe Word Search 2

```
C H W P E C T Z S R X M Q V H S C G E R
S H I E L D N E S X Q C L O N D O N S M
V S T F T A U H A X A R T O A P O I W V
M U C M T T M Q M S S E W S L T T R O X
N S H Q A Q B P T Y L A C Q S D U P R W
N A D T B S Y L S P E D H T A W R S D C
B N S O E X E U I Z D Y A T O A K T N B
W W W V P C N P R B G G H L J R I A A Q
P Z L R S M E Z H Y E P F O P F S O W K
D O Y C U L K N C P E T E R R K H C S V
W P F T Z N K O T G M V V I O N K B H J
R H N T S G R S F A A V A W F I P C Z W
X E B O R D R A W C U C D W E F F K E Y
J S T P I L U R E G S R F X S E X C F G
J R H A N N W D B E A V E R S Y I Y J D
J S L X Z L M I R Q H P G Y O M R Q H P
L P Q T N U D N D A G G E R R K B N G H
L X J X N H F E Y Y L M A U G R I M S L
J Y C D K D N S R U M B L E B U F F I N
```

A friendly giant (12)
Aslan and Peter planned this after the White Witch left camp. (6)
Aslan's breath freed these. (7)
Attacked Susan and Lucy (6)
Castle by the sea; ___ Paravel (4)
Chief of the secret police (7)
Children borrowed these from the wardrobe (5)
Doorway to Narnia (8)
Edmund broke the White Witch's (4)
Edmund's temptation: ___ Delight (7)
First to enter Narnia (4)
Half horse, half man (7)
He destroyed winter & killed the Witch. (5)
He gave useful gifts to the children: Father ___ (9)
He killed Maugrim. (5)
Home town of the Pevensie children (6)
Hunted by the adult Pevensies; White ___ (4)
It arrived with Aslan. (6)
It contained a red lion crest. (6)
It was located between two mountains: Witch's ___ (6)
Lucy met Mr. Tumnus at the ___ post. (4)
Lucy's gift that she did not use (6)
Mr. Tumnus's house was a ___. (4)
Mr. Tumnus's race (4)
Nature's white winter covering (4)
Owner of the country house where the children stayed (9)
Place of sacrifice; ___ Table (5)
She carried a horn. (5)
She told the children to stay out of trouble. (7)
She was half Jinn & half giantess; White ___ (5)
Short servant of the White Witch (5)
Sir Peter ____'s Bane (4)
Susan used this to call for help. (4)
Susan's unused gift: ___ and arrow (3)
Tea-time treat (8)
The Faun who had tea with Lucy (6)
They gnawed through Aslan's ropes. (4)
They took the children to Aslan. (7)
Used to kill Maugrim (5)
Used to save the wounded after the battle (7)
White Witch's transportation (6)
Witch used it to kill Aslan (5)
___ The Just (6)

The Lion, The Witch & The Wardrobe Word Search 2 Answer Key

A friendly giant (12)
Aslan and Peter planned this after the White Witch left camp. (6)
Aslan's breath freed these. (7)
Attacked Susan and Lucy (6)
Castle by the sea; ___ Paravel (4)
Chief of the secret police (7)
Children borrowed these from the wardrobe (5)
Doorway to Narnia (8)
Edmund broke the White Witch's (4)
Edmund's temptation: ___ Delight (7)
First to enter Narnia (4)
Half horse, half man (7)
He destroyed winter & killed the Witch. (5)
He gave useful gifts to the children: Father ___ (9)
He killed Maugrim. (5)
Home town of the Pevensie children (6)
Hunted by the adult Pevensies; White ___ (4)
It arrived with Aslan. (6)
It contained a red lion crest. (6)
It was located between two mountains: Witch's ___ (6)
Lucy met Mr. Tumnus at the ___ post. (4)

Lucy's gift that she did not use (6)
Mr. Tumnus's house was a ___. (4)
Mr. Tumnus's race (4)
Nature's white winter covering (4)
Owner of the country house where the children stayed (9)
Place of sacrifice; ___ Table (5)
She carried a horn. (5)
She told the children to stay out of trouble. (7)
She was half Jinn & half giantess; White ___ (5)
Short servant of the White Witch (5)
Sir Peter ____'s Bane (4)
Susan used this to call for help. (4)
Susan's unused gift: ___ and arrow (3)
Tea-time treat (8)
The Faun who had tea with Lucy (6)
They gnawed through Aslan's ropes. (4)
They took the children to Aslan. (7)
Used to kill Maugrim (5)
Used to save the wounded after the battle (7)
White Witch's transportation (6)
Witch used it to kill Aslan (5)
___ The Just (6)

The Lion, The Witch & The Wardrobe Word Search 3

```
D X E C H R I S T M A S D A G G E R W M
W L B C O L T A P X H Z K X S X T G O F
A M O V R A P R X R S S C M Y L W Y L Z
R A R N N M P D L A I D R O C S E Z F X
F U D C D P W I Q P K N C X E X F D R V
R G R H C O S N S H R B G U M D I H G D
U R A Z J B N E D J U O T K T J N Z L E
M I W D R O W S F S T A F G C D K W E V
B M T W G W J Z C K T K K E Q F Q L C Z
L Q J Y X X R B K S Y N D W S Q T H J M
E Y L H W S J Q M X N R P G V S C B V Y
B H Y M V R C M S Z Z N R T A K O K X W
U Y G H H K J Z N F R H B C Y W Z R S M
F M J D N M V X W B D D Q M F W X T N Z
F V G K A C W C O J K N J C R G X Q J D
I T V S S L F Q L Y S U Y R C B W R R M
N S U C L N S Z V R P M C E T A V U C Y
N W S M A D N U E K P D U A S T A Z H Y
F S T O N E W V S H I E L D S T A O C T
A N Q A R U A S C A P G T Y N L A A T X
U O W S M E S Y F X N F K E N E V G I Q
N W W O B M I C E R I A C Q R E R S W N
```

ASLAN	DAGGER	MICE	STONE
BATTLE	DWARF	PETER	SUSAN
BEAVERS	EDMUND	PROFESSOR	SWORD
BOW	FAUN	RUMBLEBUFFIN	TUMNUS
CAIR	HORN	SARDINES	TURKISH
CASTLE	KNIFE	SHIELD	WAND
CAVE	LAMP	SLEDGE	WARDROBE
CENTAUR	LONDON	SNOW	WITCH
CHRISTMAS	LUCY	SPRING	WOLF
COATS	MAUGRIM	STAG	WOLVES
CORDIAL	MCREADY	STATUES	

The Lion, The Witch & The Wardrobe Word Search 3 Answer Key

```
D       E   C H R I S T M A S D A G G E R   W
W   L   B   O   L   A   P       H       S   O
A   M   O   R   A   R   R       S       L   L
R   A   R   N   N   D   A       I   D R O C   F
R   U   D   D   M   I   L   P   K   N   E   F D G
F   G   R   P   O   N   P   R   N   G   U   I   E
U   R   A   O   N   E   L   U   O   T   E   N
M   I     W D R O W S   A   T   F     L   K   E
B   M                 S T       E     L   T
L                             S       S     O
E                                     S     R
B                                     A
U                         W   D   M   C
F               A       W O L V   C M       B
F       T       S       V   E   S N U Y C R   A     R
I       U       L       E   R   H I M P C E   T     U
N   T   M A D E U A     S H I N D Y T S A L A   H
F   S   O   N E V A S   A   E   P U L T N D E   C
A   N   O   A   U E     N   N   E L Y S   L   O T
U   O   W   W   O B M I C E R I   A   C   E     I W
N                                         R     W
```

ASLAN	DAGGER	MICE	STONE
BATTLE	DWARF	PETER	SUSAN
BEAVERS	EDMUND	PROFESSOR	SWORD
BOW	FAUN	RUMBLEBUFFIN	TUMNUS
CAIR	HORN	SARDINES	TURKISH
CASTLE	KNIFE	SHIELD	WAND
CAVE	LAMP	SLEDGE	WARDROBE
CENTAUR	LONDON	SNOW	WITCH
CHRISTMAS	LUCY	SPRING	WOLF
COATS	MAUGRIM	STAG	WOLVES
CORDIAL	MCREADY	STATUES	

The Lion, The Witch & The Wardrobe Word Search 4

```
M H V P B E A V E R S U N M U T B W C T
C S D E R W X Q X Y C G N B Z G O I O M
R N S T G O O T D F J Q M G H B W T R G
E C Z E X N F L G H P N X B S N H C D M
A T E R S S W E V M A U G R I M B H I S
D H B N K T X C S E Y L G F K S C C A R
Y R O K T X O J P S S X F Q R W E C L J
B R R N Y A B N P M O U L L U O J H F W
A C D I B W U Y E F B R J F T R D R M B
T P R F D R L R P E H Q M S K D A I W N
T G A E F M Y F L L L C Z F S W K S S Y
L X W L T Y P B R Q W Y Z N D C G T A D
E C J L Z B M F E V B L S C Z D Z M R F
T Y Y C C U D G D Q N V H K F A K A D J
X P S O R S K S M N G F I Y X G W S I K
J M T A C N L K U W L A E K H G X L N R
T A A T A A R E N W A U L R S E N G E R
E L T S A C V R D L O N D O N R N L S X
R F U L T Z I E Y G A L D V O I N U Z P
B S E R X A P G P L E P F H R M S C N V
N G S B C X G Q S K M C Q P G L B Y H B
Y B Y X J H D A T V X T S H D J C X R Y
```

ASLAN	DAGGER	MICE	STONE
BATTLE	DWARF	PETER	SUSAN
BEAVERS	EDMUND	PROFESSOR	SWORD
BOW	FAUN	RUMBLEBUFFIN	TUMNUS
CAIR	HORN	SARDINES	TURKISH
CASTLE	KNIFE	SHIELD	WAND
CAVE	LAMP	SLEDGE	WARDROBE
CENTAUR	LONDON	SNOW	WITCH
CHRISTMAS	LUCY	SPRING	WOLF
COATS	MAUGRIM	STAG	WOLVES
CORDIAL	MCREADY	STATUES	

The Lion, The Witch & The Wardrobe Word Search 4 Answer Key

```
M           P  B E A V E R S U N M U T    B   W   C
C           E  R                          O   I   O
R           T  W                      H   W   T   R
E     C     E  O                      S       C   D
A     E     R  N  F    L   M A U G R  I   N   H   I
D     B     S  S  L    E       S   F  K   M   C   A   M
Y     O     T  T  O    S       O   F  R   S   H   L
B     R     K     N    S       U      U   W   R   
A     D     N     A    E       R      T   O   I   S
T     R     I        U R              T   R   S   A
T     A     F        M L              D   D   T   R
L     W     E        B           S        W   M   D
E              C        E         H        D   A   I
               O    U   D         I   D    A   S   N
       P       A    S   M     F   E   A    G       E
       M    S  T  R   N   L   U   A   G    G       S
       A    T  S  C N A   E W U   L   E    G       
E      L    A     A V E   W N     D   N    E       
       S    T    S C  I   G  D  L O N O    R       
       U        A    E   L       D    R            
       E       C     A G S       F    H            
       S               A         S
```

ASLAN   DAGGER   MICE   STONE

BATTLE   DWARF   PETER   SUSAN

BEAVERS   EDMUND   PROFESSOR   SWORD

BOW   FAUN   RUMBLEBUFFIN   TUMNUS

CAIR   HORN   SARDINES   TURKISH

CASTLE   KNIFE   SHIELD   WAND

CAVE   LAMP   SLEDGE   WARDROBE

CENTAUR   LONDON   SNOW   WITCH

CHRISTMAS   LUCY   SPRING   WOLF

COATS   MAUGRIM   STAG   WOLVES

CORDIAL   MCREADY   STATUES

Copyrighted

The Lion, The Witch & The Wardrobe Crossword 1

Across
1. Sir Peter ____'s Bane
3. White Witch's transportation
5. He destroyed winter & killed the Witch.
7. She carried a horn.
8. Half horse, half man
13. Chief of the secret police
14. They gnawed through Aslan's ropes.
16. Castle by the sea; ____ Paravel
17. First to enter Narnia
20. Lucy's gift that she did not use
21. Nature's white winter covering
22. Lucy met Mr. Tumnus at the ____ post.
23. Susan used this to call for help.
24. It was located between two mountains: Witch's ____

Down
2. Mr. Tumnus's race
3. Hunted by the adult Pevensies; White ____
4. Short servant of the White Witch
6. The Faun who had tea with Lucy
8. Mr. Tumnus's house was a ____.
9. Edmund's temptation: ____ Delight
10. A friendly giant
11. ____ The Just
12. She was half Jinn & half giantess; White ____
15. He gave useful gifts to the children: Father ____
16. Children borrowed these from the wardrobe
17. Home town of the Pevensie children
18. He killed Maugrim.
19. Used to kill Maugrim

The Lion, The Witch & The Wardrobe Crossword 1 Answer Key

	1 W	O	L	2 F				3 S	L	E	4 D	G	E
				5 A	S	L	A	N	6 T		T		W
				U			7 S	U	S	A	N		A
		8 C	E	9 N	T	10 A	U	R		M		G		R
11 E		A		U		U		N		12 W		F
D		V		R		13 M	A	U	G	R	I	M	
14 M	15 I	C	E		K		B		A	S		T	
U		H		16 C	A	I	R		L		17 L	U	C	Y
N		R		O		S		E		O		H	
D		I		A		H		B		N			18 P
		S		T		19 S	U	20 D	A	G	G	E	R
		21 T		S	N	O	W		F		O		T
22 L	A	M	P			O		F		N		E
		A			R		I		23 H	O	R	N
24 C	A	S	T	L	E		D		N			

Across
1. Sir Peter ____'s Bane
3. White Witch's transportation
5. He destroyed winter & killed the Witch.
7. She carried a horn.
8. Half horse, half man
13. Chief of the secret police
14. They gnawed through Aslan's ropes.
16. Castle by the sea; ___ Paravel
17. First to enter Narnia
20. Lucy's gift that she did not use
21. Nature's white winter covering
22. Lucy met Mr. Tumnus at the ___ post.
23. Susan used this to call for help.
24. It was located between two mountains: Witch's ___

Down
2. Mr. Tumnus's race
3. Hunted by the adult Pevensies; White ___
4. Short servant of the White Witch
6. The Faun who had tea with Lucy
8. Mr. Tumnus's house was a ___.
9. Edmund's temptation: ___ Delight
10. A friendly giant
11. ___ The Just
12. She was half Jinn & half giantess; White ___
15. He gave useful gifts to the children: Father ___
16. Children borrowed these from the wardrobe
17. Home town of the Pevensie children
18. He killed Maugrim.
19. Used to kill Maugrim

The Lion, The Witch & The Wardrobe Crossword 2

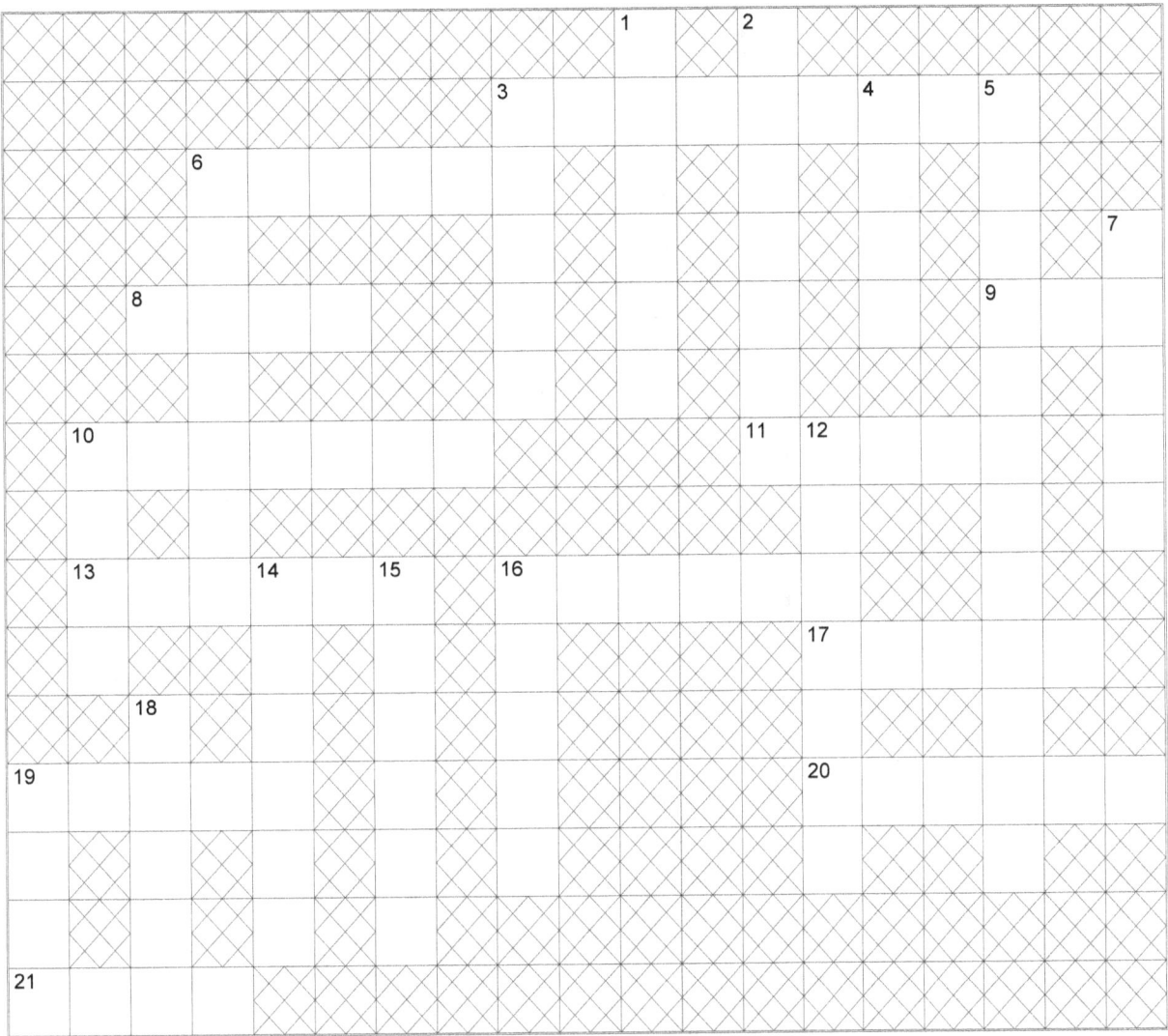

Across

3. Owner of the country house where the children stayed
6. White Witch's transportation
8. Mr. Tumnus's race
9. Susan's unused gift: ___ and arrow
10. Chief of the secret police
11. Place of sacrifice; ___ Table
13. It was located between two mountains: Witch's ___
16. Lucy's gift that she did not use
17. Witch used it to kill Aslan
19. She carried a horn.
20. It arrived with Aslan.
21. Edmund broke the White Witch's

Down

1. Attacked Susan and Lucy
2. They took the children to Aslan.
3. He killed Maugrim.
4. Hunted by the adult Pevensies; White ___
5. A friendly giant
6. Aslan's breath freed these.
7. Used to kill Maugrim
10. They gnawed through Aslan's ropes.
12. Edmund's temptation: ___ Delight
14. The Faun who had tea with Lucy
15. ___ The Just
16. Short servant of the White Witch
18. He destroyed winter & killed the Witch.
19. Nature's white winter covering

The Lion, The Witch & The Wardrobe Crossword 2 Answer Key

								¹W		²B		
					³P	R	O	F	E	S	⁴S	O	⁵R
			⁶S	L	E	D	G	E		L	A	T	U
			T		T			V		V	A		M	⁷S
		⁸F	A	U	N			E		E			⁹B	O	W
			T		R			S		R			L		O
	¹⁰M	A	U	G	R	I	M			¹¹S	¹²T	O	N	E		R
	I		E								U		B		D
	¹³C	A	¹⁴S	T	¹⁵L	E	¹⁶D	A	G	G	E	R		U	
	E		U		D		W				¹⁷K	N	I	F	E
		¹⁸A		M		M		A			I		F	
¹⁹S	U	S	A	N		U		R			²⁰S	P	R	I	N	G
N		L		U		N		F			H		N	
O		A		S		D								
²¹W	A	N	D									

Across
- 3. Owner of the country house where the children stayed
- 6. White Witch's transportation
- 8. Mr. Tumnus's race
- 9. Susan's unused gift: ___ and arrow
- 10. Chief of the secret police
- 11. Place of sacrifice; ___ Table
- 13. It was located between two mountains: Witch's ___
- 16. Lucy's gift that she did not use
- 17. Witch used it to kill Aslan
- 19. She carried a horn.
- 20. It arrived with Aslan.
- 21. Edmund broke the White Witch's

Down
- 1. Attacked Susan and Lucy
- 2. They took the children to Aslan.
- 3. He killed Maugrim.
- 4. Hunted by the adult Pevensies; White ___
- 5. A friendly giant
- 6. Aslan's breath freed these.
- 7. Used to kill Maugrim
- 10. They gnawed through Aslan's ropes.
- 12. Edmund's temptation: ___ Delight
- 14. The Faun who had tea with Lucy
- 15. ___ The Just
- 16. Short servant of the White Witch
- 18. He destroyed winter & killed the Witch.
- 19. Nature's white winter covering

The Lion, The Witch & The Wardrobe Crossword 3

Across
1. The Faun who had tea with Lucy
6. He destroyed winter & killed the Witch.
8. Short servant of the White Witch
10. Mr. Tumnus's race
11. Susan's unused gift: ___ and arrow
14. They gnawed through Aslan's ropes.
17. It arrived with Aslan.
21. Children borrowed these from the wardrobe
22. Sir Peter ____'s Bane
23. Lucy's gift that she did not use
24. Susan used this to call for help.
25. Mr. Tumnus's house was a ___.
26. Nature's white winter covering
27. First to enter Narnia

Down
1. Edmund's temptation: ___ Delight
2. Chief of the secret police
3. Tea-time treat
4. Witch used it to kill Asaln
5. ___ The Just
7. Lucy met Mr. Tumnus at the ___ post.
9. A friendly giant
12. Edmund broke the White Witch's
13. Castle by the sea; ___ Paravel
15. Home town of the Pevensie children
16. Hunted by the adult Pevensies; White ___
18. He killed Maugrim.
19. She told the children to stay out of trouble.
20. Used to kill Maugrim

The Lion, The Witch & The Wardrobe Crossword 3 Answer Key

	1 T	2 M	N	3 S		4 K	5 E		
	U	A		6 A	7 S	L	A	N	8 D	W	9 A	R	F
	R	U		R		A		I		M		U	
	K	G		D		M		10 F	A	U	N		M
	I	R		I		P		E			11 B	O	12 W
	S	I		N			13 C		D		L		A
	H	14 M	I	C	E		A				E		N
15 L		16 S		17 S	18 P	R	I	N	G		20 S	B		D
O		T		19 M		E		R				U	
N		A		21 C	O	A	T	S		22 W	O	L	F
23 D	A	G	G	E	R		E				O		F
O				E			R		24 H	O	R	N	I
N			25 C	A	V	E			D		26 S	N	O	W
				D								
		27 L	U	C	Y							

Across
1. The Faun who had tea with Lucy
6. He destroyed winter & killed the Witch.
8. Short servant of the White Witch
10. Mr. Tumnus's race
11. Susan's unused gift: ___ and arrow
14. They gnawed through Aslan's ropes.
17. It arrived with Aslan.
21. Children borrowed these from the wardrobe
22. Sir Peter ____'s Bane
23. Lucy's gift that she did not use
24. Susan used this to call for help.
25. Mr. Tumnus's house was a ___.
26. Nature's white winter covering
27. First to enter Narnia

Down
1. Edmund's temptation: ___ Delight
2. Chief of the secret police
3. Tea-time treat
4. Witch used it to kill Aslan
5. ___ The Just
7. Lucy met Mr. Tumnus at the ___ post.
9. A friendly giant
12. Edmund broke the White Witch's
13. Castle by the sea; ___ Paravel
15. Home town of the Pevensie children
16. Hunted by the adult Pevensies; White ___
18. He killed Maugrim.
19. She told the children to stay out of trouble.
20. Used to kill Maugrim

The Lion, The Witch & The Wardrobe Crossword 4

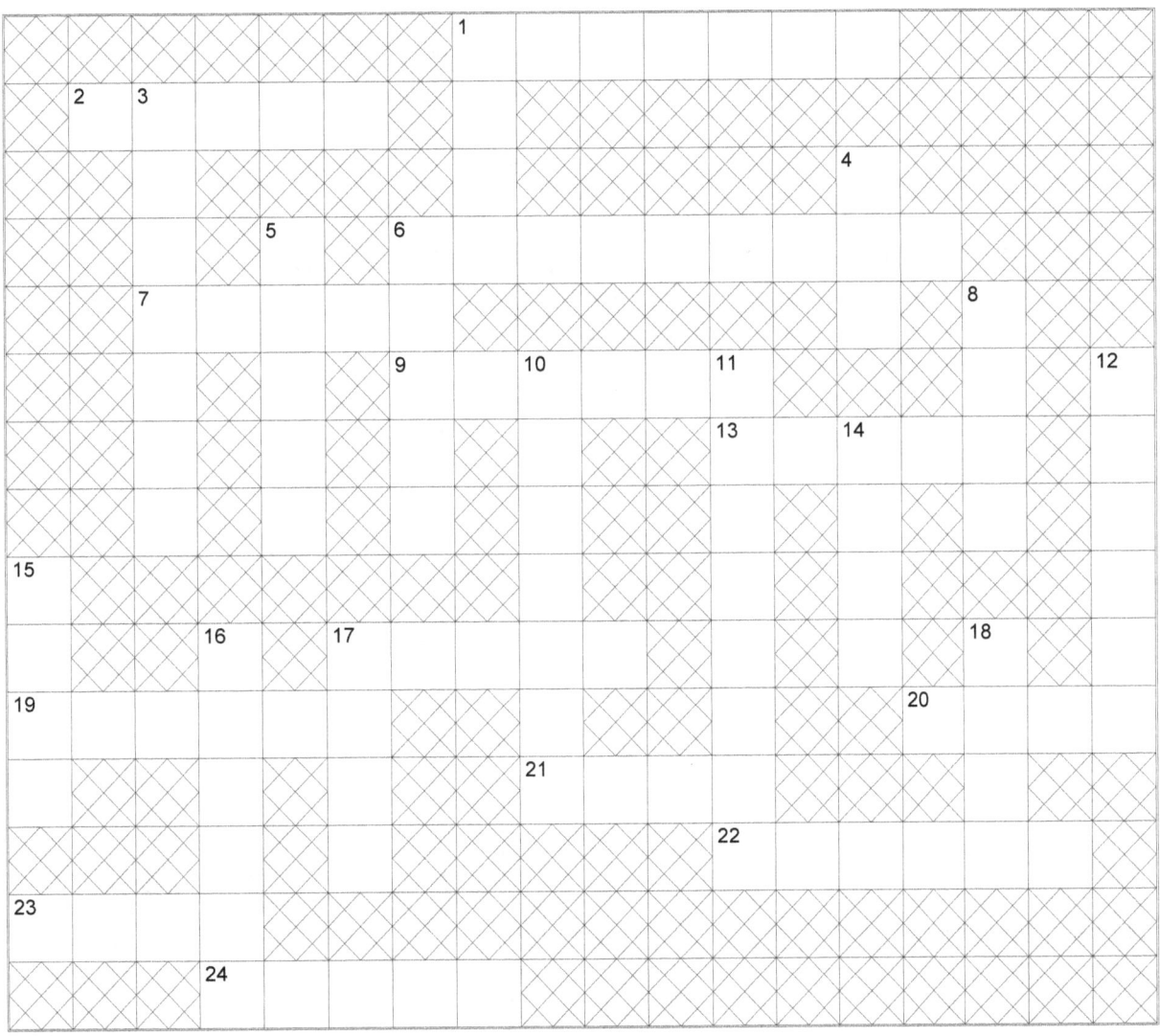

Across
1. Half horse, half man
2. Place of sacrifice; ___ Table
6. Owner of the country house where the children stayed
7. Witch used it to kill Aslan
9. The Faun who had tea with Lucy
13. He destroyed winter & killed the Witch.
17. Used to kill Maugrim
19. Home town of the Pevensie children
20. Mr. Tumnus's house was a ___.
21. They gnawed through Aslan's ropes.
22. It arrived with Aslan.
23. Susan used this to call for help.
24. Short servant of the White Witch

Down
1. Castle by the sea; ___ Paravel
3. Edmund's temptation: ___ Delight
4. Susan's unused gift: ___ and arrow
5. She was half Jinn & half giantess; White ___
6. He killed Maugrim.
8. Edmund broke the White Witch's
10. Chief of the secret police
11. Tea-time treat
12. Aslan and Peter planned this after the White Witch left camp.
14. Lucy met Mr. Tumnus at the ___ post.
15. Sir Peter ____'s Bane
16. ___ The Just
17. Nature's white winter covering
18. Mr. Tumnus's race

The Lion, The Witch & The Wardrobe Crossword 4 Answer Key

							¹C	E	N	T	A	U	R			
	² S	³ T	O	N	E		A									
		U					I						⁴ B			
		R		⁵ W		⁶ P	R	O	F	E	S	S	O	R		
		⁷ K	N	I	F	E						W		⁸ W		
		I		T		⁹ T	¹⁰ U	M	N	¹¹ U S				A		¹² B
		S		C		E	A			¹³ A S	¹⁴ L	A	N		A
		H		H		R	U			R	A		D		T
¹⁵ W							G			D	M				T
O		¹⁶ E		¹⁷ S	W	O	R	D		I		P		¹⁸ F		L
¹⁹ L	O	N	D	O	N		I			N			²⁰ C	A	V	E
F				M		O		²¹ M	I	C	E				U	
			U		W					²² S	P	R	I	N	G	
²³ H	O	R	N													
			²⁴ D	W	A	R	F									

Across
1. Half horse, half man
2. Place of sacrifice; ___ Table
6. Owner of the country house where the children stayed
7. Witch used it to kill Aslan
9. The Faun who had tea with Lucy
13. He destroyed winter & killed the Witch.
17. Used to kill Maugrim
19. Home town of the Pevensie children
20. Mr. Tumnus's house was a ___.
21. They gnawed through Aslan's ropes.
22. It arrived with Aslan.
23. Susan used this to call for help.
24. Short servant of the White Witch

Down
1. Castle by the sea; ___ Paravel
3. Edmund's temptation: ___ Delight
4. Susan's unused gift: ___ and arrow
5. She was half Jinn & half giantess; White ___
6. He killed Maugrim.
8. Edmund broke the White Witch's
10. Chief of the secret police
11. Tea-time treat
12. Aslan and Peter planned this after the White Witch left camp.
14. Lucy met Mr. Tumnus at the ___ post.
15. Sir Peter ___'s Bane
16. ___ The Just
17. Nature's white winter covering
18. Mr. Tumnus's race

Lion, Witch & Wardrobe

SHIELD	STATUES	CENTAUR	CAIR	PETER
WARDROBE	MCREADY	WITCH	CHRISTMAS	EDMUND
SLEDGE	STAG	FREE SPACE	BATTLE	DAGGER
SARDINES	CAVE	MICE	STONE	SPRING
PROFESSOR	LAMP	BEAVERS	WOLVES	RUMBLEBUFFIN

Lion, Witch & Wardrobe

FAUN	DWARF	TURKISH	LUCY	MAUGRIM
SWORD	COATS	BOW	WAND	LONDON
SUSAN	CASTLE	FREE SPACE	TUMNUS	SNOW
CORDIAL	ASLAN	KNIFE	RUMBLEBUFFIN	WOLVES
BEAVERS	LAMP	PROFESSOR	SPRING	STONE

Lion, Witch & Wardrobe

STATUES	WOLVES	ASLAN	WITCH	SUSAN
BOW	MICE	STAG	DWARF	DAGGER
STONE	CORDIAL	FREE SPACE	TUMNUS	CAVE
CHRISTMAS	LONDON	TURKISH	COATS	KNIFE
PROFESSOR	MCREADY	FAUN	HORN	SPRING

Lion, Witch & Wardrobe

EDMUND	PETER	SWORD	SNOW	CAIR
BEAVERS	SLEDGE	RUMBLEBUFFIN	SHIELD	LAMP
MAUGRIM	BATTLE	FREE SPACE	CASTLE	WOLF
SARDINES	LUCY	WARDROBE	SPRING	HORN
FAUN	MCREADY	PROFESSOR	KNIFE	COATS

Lion, Witch & Wardrobe

CASTLE	CORDIAL	LAMP	PETER	CAIR
SUSAN	SWORD	COATS	CAVE	BATTLE
LONDON	SHIELD	FREE SPACE	ASLAN	BOW
DWARF	FAUN	SNOW	MAUGRIM	SARDINES
STONE	CENTAUR	PROFESSOR	DAGGER	EDMUND

Lion, Witch & Wardrobe

TUMNUS	HORN	RUMBLEBUFFIN	MCREADY	STATUES
LUCY	BEAVERS	WOLVES	WAND	TURKISH
STAG	MICE	FREE SPACE	CHRISTMAS	SLEDGE
WARDROBE	KNIFE	WOLF	EDMUND	DAGGER
PROFESSOR	CENTAUR	STONE	SARDINES	MAUGRIM

Lion, Witch & Wardrobe

SPRING	MICE	WITCH	CASTLE	SNOW
CORDIAL	PROFESSOR	SUSAN	RUMBLEBUFFIN	CENTAUR
HORN	TURKISH	FREE SPACE	BATTLE	FAUN
LONDON	ASLAN	KNIFE	CAVE	BOW
MAUGRIM	PETER	STAG	COATS	LUCY

Lion, Witch & Wardrobe

SARDINES	WOLVES	TUMNUS	SHIELD	EDMUND
SLEDGE	LAMP	WOLF	SWORD	CAIR
BEAVERS	CHRISTMAS	FREE SPACE	WAND	STATUES
WARDROBE	STONE	DAGGER	LUCY	COATS
STAG	PETER	MAUGRIM	BOW	CAVE

Lion, Witch & Wardrobe

PETER	STONE	CAVE	LAMP	WAND
WITCH	LONDON	TURKISH	ASLAN	WOLF
BATTLE	LUCY	FREE SPACE	CAIR	MCREADY
DWARF	SARDINES	SUSAN	BOW	FAUN
DAGGER	KNIFE	MICE	RUMBLEBUFFIN	CORDIAL

Lion, Witch & Wardrobe

STAG	HORN	WOLVES	SHIELD	BEAVERS
CENTAUR	TUMNUS	SNOW	STATUES	PROFESSOR
CHRISTMAS	SPRING	FREE SPACE	EDMUND	SLEDGE
SWORD	MAUGRIM	WARDROBE	CORDIAL	RUMBLEBUFFIN
MICE	KNIFE	DAGGER	FAUN	BOW

Lion, Witch & Wardrobe

TUMNUS	STONE	DAGGER	CAIR	SPRING
BATTLE	CENTAUR	STAG	BEAVERS	RUMBLEBUFFIN
PROFESSOR	MICE	FREE SPACE	LAMP	WOLVES
BOW	WOLF	SUSAN	STATUES	MAUGRIM
PETER	SLEDGE	HORN	SNOW	SARDINES

Lion, Witch & Wardrobe

CORDIAL	SHIELD	FAUN	COATS	CASTLE
EDMUND	CAVE	KNIFE	TURKISH	CHRISTMAS
ASLAN	LUCY	FREE SPACE	WARDROBE	WITCH
DWARF	LONDON	WAND	SARDINES	SNOW
HORN	SLEDGE	PETER	MAUGRIM	STATUES

Lion, Witch & Wardrobe

STAG	TUMNUS	SNOW	WOLVES	COATS
HORN	SPRING	WITCH	TURKISH	FAUN
PETER	CENTAUR	FREE SPACE	WARDROBE	STONE
SWORD	BOW	WAND	MAUGRIM	PROFESSOR
CAVE	CASTLE	BEAVERS	DAGGER	SLEDGE

Lion, Witch & Wardrobe

DWARF	WOLF	LUCY	EDMUND	STATUES
KNIFE	MICE	SARDINES	LONDON	LAMP
CAIR	MCREADY	FREE SPACE	ASLAN	CHRISTMAS
CORDIAL	SUSAN	BATTLE	SLEDGE	DAGGER
BEAVERS	CASTLE	CAVE	PROFESSOR	MAUGRIM

Lion, Witch & Wardrobe

STONE	STAG	KNIFE	SUSAN	ASLAN
LONDON	BOW	CASTLE	CAVE	MAUGRIM
DAGGER	WOLF	FREE SPACE	SNOW	TURKISH
MICE	FAUN	BEAVERS	COATS	BATTLE
WITCH	SPRING	EDMUND	CENTAUR	CHRISTMAS

Lion, Witch & Wardrobe

STATUES	LUCY	RUMBLEBUFFIN	WOLVES	TUMNUS
SWORD	PETER	SHIELD	HORN	PROFESSOR
LAMP	CAIR	FREE SPACE	MCREADY	WAND
DWARF	SARDINES	CORDIAL	CHRISTMAS	CENTAUR
EDMUND	SPRING	WITCH	BATTLE	COATS

Lion, Witch & Wardrobe

SPRING	COATS	MICE	DAGGER	MAUGRIM
CHRISTMAS	STAG	WARDROBE	SNOW	CAIR
BOW	WOLVES	FREE SPACE	PROFESSOR	FAUN
HORN	RUMBLEBUFFIN	LAMP	CAVE	WAND
LUCY	MCREADY	CENTAUR	ASLAN	STONE

Lion, Witch & Wardrobe

DWARF	TUMNUS	WOLF	BATTLE	KNIFE
WITCH	SUSAN	SARDINES	TURKISH	SWORD
EDMUND	BEAVERS	FREE SPACE	SHIELD	SLEDGE
LONDON	CASTLE	CORDIAL	STONE	ASLAN
CENTAUR	MCREADY	LUCY	WAND	CAVE

Lion, Witch & Wardrobe

TUMNUS	BEAVERS	SHIELD	BOW	LAMP
MICE	LUCY	RUMBLEBUFFIN	CHRISTMAS	STONE
HORN	PETER	FREE SPACE	DAGGER	SLEDGE
BATTLE	STATUES	PROFESSOR	EDMUND	CASTLE
WAND	STAG	WOLVES	SUSAN	KNIFE

Lion, Witch & Wardrobe

SNOW	TURKISH	CENTAUR	CAVE	SARDINES
SWORD	LONDON	SPRING	CAIR	MAUGRIM
WOLF	DWARF	FREE SPACE	FAUN	WARDROBE
ASLAN	COATS	CORDIAL	KNIFE	SUSAN
WOLVES	STAG	WAND	CASTLE	EDMUND

Lion, Witch & Wardrobe

BATTLE	WITCH	FAUN	STAG	KNIFE
MICE	CORDIAL	STONE	PROFESSOR	SLEDGE
ASLAN	SPRING	FREE SPACE	WOLVES	SNOW
MAUGRIM	BEAVERS	CHRISTMAS	HORN	MCREADY
LAMP	TURKISH	SHIELD	TUMNUS	CENTAUR

Lion, Witch & Wardrobe

CASTLE	WARDROBE	DAGGER	SUSAN	SARDINES
CAIR	PETER	WOLF	CAVE	RUMBLEBUFFIN
SWORD	LONDON	FREE SPACE	WAND	BOW
COATS	STATUES	LUCY	CENTAUR	TUMNUS
SHIELD	TURKISH	LAMP	MCREADY	HORN

Lion, Witch & Wardrobe

TUMNUS	STAG	COATS	LUCY	CAVE
FAUN	CORDIAL	SHIELD	WOLF	DWARF
EDMUND	DAGGER	FREE SPACE	MAUGRIM	STATUES
CAIR	HORN	CHRISTMAS	SWORD	SPRING
CENTAUR	BOW	SUSAN	SLEDGE	BEAVERS

Lion, Witch & Wardrobe

STONE	WITCH	WOLVES	PROFESSOR	ASLAN
SARDINES	WAND	SNOW	TURKISH	RUMBLEBUFFIN
BATTLE	LONDON	FREE SPACE	CASTLE	WARDROBE
KNIFE	LAMP	MCREADY	BEAVERS	SLEDGE
SUSAN	BOW	CENTAUR	SPRING	SWORD

Lion, Witch & Wardrobe

CENTAUR	TUMNUS	DAGGER	FAUN	BEAVERS
STONE	SNOW	SARDINES	LUCY	STATUES
TURKISH	SLEDGE	FREE SPACE	BATTLE	LAMP
ASLAN	SUSAN	SHIELD	CAIR	PROFESSOR
SPRING	SWORD	HORN	WOLF	CHRISTMAS

Lion, Witch & Wardrobe

KNIFE	CAVE	WOLVES	COATS	WARDROBE
WITCH	CORDIAL	MCREADY	PETER	EDMUND
STAG	CASTLE	FREE SPACE	MICE	BOW
DWARF	MAUGRIM	WAND	CHRISTMAS	WOLF
HORN	SWORD	SPRING	PROFESSOR	CAIR

Lion, Witch & Wardrobe

SARDINES	FAUN	SWORD	SPRING	EDMUND
SUSAN	CASTLE	HORN	KNIFE	PROFESSOR
CENTAUR	WOLF	FREE SPACE	BOW	SNOW
CAVE	CORDIAL	DWARF	MCREADY	STAG
LUCY	STONE	DAGGER	CAIR	BATTLE

Lion, Witch & Wardrobe

BEAVERS	WAND	LAMP	CHRISTMAS	WARDROBE
COATS	STATUES	ASLAN	TURKISH	RUMBLEBUFFIN
SHIELD	WITCH	FREE SPACE	WOLVES	TUMNUS
MICE	MAUGRIM	LONDON	BATTLE	CAIR
DAGGER	STONE	LUCY	STAG	MCREADY

Lion, Witch & Wardrobe

SARDINES	DAGGER	EDMUND	LUCY	SLEDGE
SUSAN	BEAVERS	WOLF	SNOW	WARDROBE
FAUN	SPRING	FREE SPACE	MICE	WITCH
HORN	WOLVES	MCREADY	PETER	RUMBLEBUFFIN
KNIFE	WAND	CAVE	COATS	MAUGRIM

Lion, Witch & Wardrobe

STONE	CENTAUR	SHIELD	SWORD	LONDON
CHRISTMAS	TURKISH	CORDIAL	ASLAN	BATTLE
DWARF	PROFESSOR	FREE SPACE	CAIR	CASTLE
BOW	STAG	STATUES	MAUGRIM	COATS
CAVE	WAND	KNIFE	RUMBLEBUFFIN	PETER

Lion, Witch & Wardrobe

PETER	SNOW	FAUN	MCREADY	SUSAN
BATTLE	MAUGRIM	LONDON	LUCY	DWARF
DAGGER	MICE	FREE SPACE	CASTLE	RUMBLEBUFFIN
CENTAUR	TURKISH	SLEDGE	STATUES	STAG
CORDIAL	KNIFE	CHRISTMAS	WAND	BOW

Lion, Witch & Wardrobe

STONE	BEAVERS	WOLVES	COATS	CAVE
SHIELD	LAMP	WITCH	ASLAN	WARDROBE
SWORD	EDMUND	FREE SPACE	PROFESSOR	TUMNUS
WOLF	SARDINES	HORN	BOW	WAND
CHRISTMAS	KNIFE	CORDIAL	STAG	STATUES

The Lion, The Witch & The Wardrobe Vocabulary Word List

No.	Word	Clue/Definition
1.	ABIDE	Put up with; tolerate
2.	ALIGHTING	Coming down and settling, as after flight
3.	ALLIANCE	Political partnership
4.	BANE	Cause of harm, ruin, or death
5.	BEASTLY	Very disagreeable; unpleasant
6.	BECKONED	Signaled or summoned, as by nodding or waving
7.	BOUGHS	Tree branches, especially large or main branches
8.	BRISTLING	Standing stiffly on end
9.	BURRING	A buzzing or whirring sound
10.	CAMPAIGN	Military operation or plan
11.	CAMPHOR	Compound made of bark and leaves, used to repel insects
12.	CENTAUR	Mythical being that is half man and half horse
13.	CORDIAL	Invigorating & stimulating tonic
14.	DECOY	Something used to lure victims into danger
15.	DIN	Loud, harsh noise
16.	DISPOSAL	To allow one to use or be of service to another
17.	DOMINION	Territory of influence or control; realm
18.	DRATTED	Frustrating; cursed
19.	ENCHANTED	Influenced by charms or spells
20.	FESTOONS	Decorative garlands of flowers or leaves
21.	FOREBODING	Sense of impending evil or misfortune
22.	FRATERNIZING	Associating with others in a brotherly way
23.	GAIETY	State of joyful exuberance or merriment
24.	GIBBER	Rapidly speak about unimportant matters
25.	GLADE	Open space in a forest
26.	GLUTTONY	Excess in eating or drinking
27.	HEARTILY	With warmth and sincerity
28.	HOAX	An act intended to deceive or trick
29.	INCANTATION	Words believed to have a magical effect; a spell
30.	INQUISITIVE	Inclined to investigate; eager for knowledge
31.	JEERING	Verbal abuse; taunting
32.	JOLLIFICATION	Festivity; revelry
33.	LABURNUM	Kind of tree with clusters of yellow flowers
34.	LARDER	Place, such as a pantry or cellar, where food is stored
35.	LEERING	Look with a sidelong glance with evil intent
36.	LITHE	Gracefully slender; moving and blending with ease
37.	LULLING	Soothing; calming; causing to sleep or rest
38.	MANTLE	Loose, sleeveless coat worn over outer garments; cloak
39.	MELANCHOLY	Sadness or depression of the spirits
40.	MUFFLER	Heavy scarf worn around the neck for warmth
41.	ORDINARY	Of no exceptional ability
42.	PARCELS	Packages; wrapped-up items
43.	PAVILION	Ornate tent
44.	PEDLARS	British word for one who travels about selling wares
45.	PREMISES	A building and its surrounding grounds
46.	PRODIGIOUS	Impressively great in size or force
47.	PROPHECY	Prediction of the future
48.	QUARRY	Prey; a hunted animal
49.	RABBLE	Disorderly crowd of people
50.	RECKONED	Relied on with confidence
51.	REMNANTS	Left-overs

The Lion, The Witch & The Wardrobe Vocabulary Word List Continued

No. Word	Clue/Definition
52. RENOUNCED	Given up, especially by formal announcement
53. REPULSIVE	Offensive or disgusting
54. RESUMED	Began again; continued after interruption
55. SATYR	Mythological creature composed of part man and part goat
56. SHORN	Shaved
57. SHRILL	High-pitched and piercing in tone or sound
58. SLEDGE	Vehicle mounted on runners, drawn by work animals across ice
59. SLUICE	Kind of gate that controls the rate of water flow through a channel
60. SNAPPISHLY	In an irritable and short-tempered manner
61. SNIGGER	A disrespectful laugh
62. SOLEMN	Deeply earnest, serious, and sober
63. SPIRES	Structures that taper to a point at the top
64. SPITEFUL	Showing ill will and a desire to hurt
65. SPRINGY	Elastic, soft, bouncy
66. STAG	The adult male of various deer
67. STRATAGEM	Military plan designed to deceive or surprise an enemy
68. SULKY	Pouting and withdrawn
69. TOKEN	Something serving as proof of something else; a sign
70. TREACHEROUS	Not to be relied on; not dependable or trustworthy; dangerous
71. TRIFLE	Something of little importance or value
72. TROOPED	Moved as a group
73. TURRET	Small tower extending above a building
74. VELVET	Cover over with a soft, furry covering
75. VENTURED	Took a risk; dared
76. VERMIN	Pests; people considered hateful or highly offensive
77. WARDROBE	Tall cabinet or closet built to hold clothes
78. WHET	Sharpen
79. WRETCHED	Of a poor or mean character

The Lion, The Witch & The Wardrobe Vocabulary Fill In The Blanks 1

1. Tall cabinet or closet built to hold clothes
2. Not to be relied on; not dependable or trustworthy; dangerous
3. Compound made of bark and leaves, used to repel insects
4. Given up, especially by formal announcement
5. A disrespectful laugh
6. Impressively great in size or force
7. Gracefully slender; moving and blending with ease
8. Military plan designed to deceive or surprise an enemy
9. An act intended to deceive or trick
10. Something of little importance or value
11. Influenced by charms or spells
12. Associating with others in a brotherly way
13. Small tower extending above a building
14. Offensive or disgusting
15. Kind of gate that controls the rate of water flow through a channel
16. Decorative garlands of flowers or leaves
17. Standing stiffly on end
18. Put up with; tolerate
19. Showing ill will and a desire to hurt
20. A buzzing or whirring sound

The Lion, The Witch & The Wardrobe Vocabulary Fill In The Blanks 1 Answer Key

WARDROBE	1. Tall cabinet or closet built to hold clothes
TREACHEROUS	2. Not to be relied on; not dependable or trustworthy; dangerous
CAMPHOR	3. Compound made of bark and leaves, used to repel insects
RENOUNCED	4. Given up, especially by formal announcement
SNIGGER	5. A disrespectful laugh
PRODIGIOUS	6. Impressively great in size or force
LITHE	7. Gracefully slender; moving and blending with ease
STRATAGEM	8. Military plan designed to deceive or surprise an enemy
HOAX	9. An act intended to deceive or trick
TRIFLE	10. Something of little importance or value
ENCHANTED	11. Influenced by charms or spells
FRATERNIZING	12. Associating with others in a brotherly way
TURRET	13. Small tower extending above a building
REPULSIVE	14. Offensive or disgusting
SLUICE	15. Kind of gate that controls the rate of water flow through a channel
FESTOONS	16. Decorative garlands of flowers or leaves
BRISTLING	17. Standing stiffly on end
ABIDE	18. Put up with; tolerate
SPITEFUL	19. Showing ill will and a desire to hurt
BURRING	20. A buzzing or whirring sound

The Lion, The Witch & The Wardrobe Vocabulary Fill In The Blanks 2

_____ 1. Structures that taper to a point at the top

_____ 2. Look with a sidelong glance with evil intent

_____ 3. Gracefully slender; moving and blending with ease

_____ 4. Festivity; revelry

_____ 5. British word for one who travels about selling wares

_____ 6. Place, such as a pantry or cellar, where food is stored

_____ 7. Disorderly crowd of people

_____ 8. Loose, sleeveless coat worn over outer garments; cloak

_____ 9. Vehicle mounted on runners, drawn by work animals across ice

_____ 10. Loud, harsh noise

_____ 11. Put up with; tolerate

_____ 12. Impressively great in size or force

_____ 13. Open space in a forest

_____ 14. Of no exceptional ability

_____ 15. Prey; a hunted animal

_____ 16. High-pitched and piercing in tone or sound

_____ 17. Very disagreeable; unpleasant

_____ 18. A disrespectful laugh

_____ 19. Invigorating & stimulating tonic

_____ 20. Territory of influence or control; realm

The Lion, The Witch & The Wardrobe Vocabulary Fill In The Blanks 2 Answer Key

SPIRES	1. Structures that taper to a point at the top
LEERING	2. Look with a sidelong glance with evil intent
LITHE	3. Gracefully slender; moving and blending with ease
JOLLIFICATION	4. Festivity; revelry
PEDLARS	5. British word for one who travels about selling wares
LARDER	6. Place, such as a pantry or cellar, where food is stored
RABBLE	7. Disorderly crowd of people
MANTLE	8. Loose, sleeveless coat worn over outer garments; cloak
SLEDGE	9. Vehicle mounted on runners, drawn by work animals across ice
DIN	10. Loud, harsh noise
ABIDE	11. Put up with; tolerate
PRODIGIOUS	12. Impressively great in size or force
GLADE	13. Open space in a forest
ORDINARY	14. Of no exceptional ability
QUARRY	15. Prey; a hunted animal
SHRILL	16. High-pitched and piercing in tone or sound
BEASTLY	17. Very disagreeable; unpleasant
SNIGGER	18. A disrespectful laugh
CORDIAL	19. Invigorating & stimulating tonic
DOMINION	20. Territory of influence or control; realm

Copyrighted

The Lion, The Witch & The Wardrobe Vocabulary Fill In The Blanks 3

_____ 1. Sadness or depression of the spirits

_____ 2. Vehicle mounted on runners, drawn by work animals across ice

_____ 3. Cause of harm, ruin, or death

_____ 4. Mythological creature composed of part man and part goat

_____ 5. Elastic, soft, bouncy

_____ 6. Showing ill will and a desire to hurt

_____ 7. Military operation or plan

_____ 8. Decorative garlands of flowers or leaves

_____ 9. Very disagreeable; unpleasant

_____ 10. Territory of influence or control; realm

_____ 11. Coming down and settling, as after flight

_____ 12. Pests; people considered hateful or highly offensive

_____ 13. Prey; a hunted animal

_____ 14. A building and its surrounding grounds

_____ 15. Pouting and withdrawn

_____ 16. Invigorating & stimulating tonic

_____ 17. Open space in a forest

_____ 18. Frustrating; cursed

_____ 19. Words believed to have a magical effect; a spell

_____ 20. A buzzing or whirring sound

The Lion, The Witch & The Wardrobe Vocabulary Fill In The Blanks 3 Answer Key

MELANCHOLY	1. Sadness or depression of the spirits
SLEDGE	2. Vehicle mounted on runners, drawn by work animals across ice
BANE	3. Cause of harm, ruin, or death
SATYR	4. Mythological creature composed of part man and part goat
SPRINGY	5. Elastic, soft, bouncy
SPITEFUL	6. Showing ill will and a desire to hurt
CAMPAIGN	7. Military operation or plan
FESTOONS	8. Decorative garlands of flowers or leaves
BEASTLY	9. Very disagreeable; unpleasant
DOMINION	10. Territory of influence or control; realm
ALIGHTING	11. Coming down and settling, as after flight
VERMIN	12. Pests; people considered hateful or highly offensive
QUARRY	13. Prey; a hunted animal
PREMISES	14. A building and its surrounding grounds
SULKY	15. Pouting and withdrawn
CORDIAL	16. Invigorating & stimulating tonic
GLADE	17. Open space in a forest
DRATTED	18. Frustrating; cursed
INCANTATION	19. Words believed to have a magical effect; a spell
BURRING	20. A buzzing or whirring sound

The Lion, The Witch & The Wardrobe Vocabulary Fill In The Blanks 4

_____ 1. Small tower extending above a building

_____ 2. Not to be relied on; not dependable or trustworthy; dangerous

_____ 3. Place, such as a pantry or cellar, where food is stored

_____ 4. Decorative garlands of flowers or leaves

_____ 5. Relied on with confidence

_____ 6. Showing ill will and a desire to hurt

_____ 7. Offensive or disgusting

_____ 8. Sense of impending evil or misfortune

_____ 9. Gracefully slender; moving and blending with ease

_____ 10. Compound made of bark and leaves, used to repel insects

_____ 11. Something serving as proof of something else; a sign

_____ 12. A building and its surrounding grounds

_____ 13. Tree branches, especially large or main branches

_____ 14. A buzzing or whirring sound

_____ 15. Military plan designed to deceive or surprise an enemy

_____ 16. Soothing; calming; causing to sleep or rest

_____ 17. Moved as a group

_____ 18. Given up, especially by formal announcement

_____ 19. Put up with; tolerate

_____ 20. Cause of harm, ruin, or death

The Lion, The Witch & The Wardrobe Vocabulary Fill In The Blanks 4 Answer Key

TURRET	1. Small tower extending above a building
TREACHEROUS	2. Not to be relied on; not dependable or trustworthy; dangerous
LARDER	3. Place, such as a pantry or cellar, where food is stored
FESTOONS	4. Decorative garlands of flowers or leaves
RECKONED	5. Relied on with confidence
SPITEFUL	6. Showing ill will and a desire to hurt
REPULSIVE	7. Offensive or disgusting
FOREBODING	8. Sense of impending evil or misfortune
LITHE	9. Gracefully slender; moving and blending with ease
CAMPHOR	10. Compound made of bark and leaves, used to repel insects
TOKEN	11. Something serving as proof of something else; a sign
PREMISES	12. A building and its surrounding grounds
BOUGHS	13. Tree branches, especially large or main branches
BURRING	14. A buzzing or whirring sound
STRATAGEM	15. Military plan designed to deceive or surprise an enemy
LULLING	16. Soothing; calming; causing to sleep or rest
TROOPED	17. Moved as a group
RENOUNCED	18. Given up, especially by formal announcement
ABIDE	19. Put up with; tolerate
BANE	20. Cause of harm, ruin, or death

The Lion, The Witch & The Wardrobe Vocabulary Matching 1

___ 1. HOAX   A. Sharpen
___ 2. SHRILL   B. Look with a sidelong glance with evil intent
___ 3. PAVILION   C. Military operation or plan
___ 4. SLEDGE   D. Structures that taper to a point at the top
___ 5. MUFFLER   E. Ornate tent
___ 6. RESUMED   F. Associating with others in a brotherly way
___ 7. DISPOSAL   G. Heavy scarf worn around the neck for warmth
___ 8. RABBLE   H. An act intended to deceive or trick
___ 9. ORDINARY   I. Territory of influence or control; realm
___10. FRATERNIZING J. A buzzing or whirring sound
___11. BECKONED   K. Of no exceptional ability
___12. STRATAGEM   L. Shaved
___13. LEERING   M. Signaled or summoned, as by nodding or waving
___14. WHET   N. Disorderly crowd of people
___15. LULLING   O. Something of little importance or value
___16. ALLIANCE   P. Prediction of the future
___17. PROPHECY   Q. Political partnership
___18. QUARRY   R. High-pitched and piercing in tone or sound
___19. SHORN   S. Vehicle mounted on runners, drawn by work animals across ice
___20. SPRINGY   T. Began again; continued after interruption
___21. TRIFLE   U. Elastic, soft, bouncy
___22. SPIRES   V. Soothing; calming; causing to sleep or rest
___23. BURRING   W. To allow one to use or be of service to another
___24. DOMINION   X. Military plan designed to deceive or surprise an enemy
___25. CAMPAIGN   Y. Prey; a hunted animal

The Lion, The Witch & The Wardrobe Vocabulary Matching 1 Answer Key

H - 1.	HOAX	A. Sharpen
R - 2.	SHRILL	B. Look with a sidelong glance with evil intent
E - 3.	PAVILION	C. Military operation or plan
S - 4.	SLEDGE	D. Structures that taper to a point at the top
G - 5.	MUFFLER	E. Ornate tent
T - 6.	RESUMED	F. Associating with others in a brotherly way
W - 7.	DISPOSAL	G. Heavy scarf worn around the neck for warmth
N - 8.	RABBLE	H. An act intended to deceive or trick
K - 9.	ORDINARY	I. Territory of influence or control; realm
F - 10.	FRATERNIZING	J. A buzzing or whirring sound
M - 11.	BECKONED	K. Of no exceptional ability
X - 12.	STRATAGEM	L. Shaved
B - 13.	LEERING	M. Signaled or summoned, as by nodding or waving
A - 14.	WHET	N. Disorderly crowd of people
V - 15.	LULLING	O. Something of little importance or value
Q - 16.	ALLIANCE	P. Prediction of the future
P - 17.	PROPHECY	Q. Political partnership
Y - 18.	QUARRY	R. High-pitched and piercing in tone or sound
L - 19.	SHORN	S. Vehicle mounted on runners, drawn by work animals across ice
U - 20.	SPRINGY	T. Began again; continued after interruption
O - 21.	TRIFLE	U. Elastic, soft, bouncy
D - 22.	SPIRES	V. Soothing; calming; causing to sleep or rest
J - 23.	BURRING	W. To allow one to use or be of service to another
I - 24.	DOMINION	X. Military plan designed to deceive or surprise an enemy
C - 25.	CAMPAIGN	Y. Prey; a hunted animal

The Lion, The Witch & The Wardrobe Vocabulary Matching 2

___ 1. PRODIGIOUS   A. Not to be relied on; not dependable or trustworthy; dangerous
___ 2. TREACHEROUS   B. Inclined to investigate; eager for knowledge
___ 3. BEASTLY   C. Began again; continued after interruption
___ 4. RESUMED   D. Relied on with confidence
___ 5. ALIGHTING   E. Loose, sleeveless coat worn over outer garments; cloak
___ 6. ENCHANTED   F. Kind of gate that controls the rate of water flow through a channel
___ 7. FESTOONS   G. Kind of tree with clusters of yellow flowers
___ 8. PARCELS   H. Rapidly speak about unimportant matters
___ 9. LABURNUM   I. Decorative garlands of flowers or leaves
___10. RECKONED   J. Packages; wrapped-up items
___11. LITHE   K. Influenced by charms or spells
___12. MANTLE   L. A disrespectful laugh
___13. PAVILION   M. Coming down and settling, as after flight
___14. GIBBER   N. Very disagreeable; unpleasant
___15. LARDER   O. Place, such as a pantry or cellar, where food is stored
___16. WRETCHED   P. Impressively great in size or force
___17. HOAX   Q. To allow one to use or be of service to another
___18. PROPHECY   R. Of a poor or mean character
___19. ALLIANCE   S. An act intended to deceive or trick
___20. SHORN   T. Gracefully slender; moving and blending with ease
___21. SLUICE   U. Took a risk; dared
___22. SNIGGER   V. Ornate tent
___23. INQUISITIVE   W. Political partnership
___24. VENTURED   X. Prediction of the future
___25. DISPOSAL   Y. Shaved

The Lion, The Witch & The Wardrobe Vocabulary Matching 2 Answer Key

P - 1. PRODIGIOUS	A.	Not to be relied on; not dependable or trustworthy; dangerous
A - 2. TREACHEROUS	B.	Inclined to investigate; eager for knowledge
N - 3. BEASTLY	C.	Began again; continued after interruption
C - 4. RESUMED	D.	Relied on with confidence
M - 5. ALIGHTING	E.	Loose, sleeveless coat worn over outer garments; cloak
K - 6. ENCHANTED	F.	Kind of gate that controls the rate of water flow through a channel
I - 7. FESTOONS	G.	Kind of tree with clusters of yellow flowers
J - 8. PARCELS	H.	Rapidly speak about unimportant matters
G - 9. LABURNUM	I.	Decorative garlands of flowers or leaves
D - 10. RECKONED	J.	Packages; wrapped-up items
T - 11. LITHE	K.	Influenced by charms or spells
E - 12. MANTLE	L.	A disrespectful laugh
V - 13. PAVILION	M.	Coming down and settling, as after flight
H - 14. GIBBER	N.	Very disagreeable; unpleasant
O - 15. LARDER	O.	Place, such as a pantry or cellar, where food is stored
R - 16. WRETCHED	P.	Impressively great in size or force
S - 17. HOAX	Q.	To allow one to use or be of service to another
X - 18. PROPHECY	R.	Of a poor or mean character
W - 19. ALLIANCE	S.	An act intended to deceive or trick
Y - 20. SHORN	T.	Gracefully slender; moving and blending with ease
F - 21. SLUICE	U.	Took a risk; dared
L - 22. SNIGGER	V.	Ornate tent
B - 23. INQUISITIVE	W.	Political partnership
U - 24. VENTURED	X.	Prediction of the future
Q - 25. DISPOSAL	Y.	Shaved

The Lion, The Witch & The Wardrobe Vocabulary Matching 3

___ 1. VERMIN
___ 2. SATYR
___ 3. CENTAUR
___ 4. PREMISES
___ 5. SLUICE
___ 6. RENOUNCED
___ 7. BANE
___ 8. GAIETY
___ 9. SLEDGE
___ 10. SPRINGY
___ 11. TOKEN
___ 12. PARCELS
___ 13. PRODIGIOUS
___ 14. TROOPED
___ 15. SHRILL
___ 16. LABURNUM
___ 17. MANTLE
___ 18. BOUGHS
___ 19. LARDER
___ 20. LITHE
___ 21. SNIGGER
___ 22. DRATTED
___ 23. TURRET
___ 24. TRIFLE
___ 25. SULKY

A. Frustrating; cursed
B. Kind of gate that controls the rate of water flow through a channel
C. Elastic, soft, bouncy
D. Moved as a group
E. Tree branches, especially large or main branches
F. Small tower extending above a building
G. High-pitched and piercing in tone or sound
H. Given up, especially by formal announcement
I. Loose, sleeveless coat worn over outer garments; cloak
J. State of joyful exuberance or merriment
K. A building and its surrounding grounds
L. Packages; wrapped-up items
M. Place, such as a pantry or cellar, where food is stored
N. Kind of tree with clusters of yellow flowers
O. Mythological creature composed of part man and part goat
P. Gracefully slender; moving and blending with ease
Q. Mythical being that is half man and half horse
R. A disrespectful laugh
S. Something serving as proof of something else; a sign
T. Pouting and withdrawn
U. Vehicle mounted on runners, drawn by work animals across ice
V. Impressively great in size or force
W. Pests; people considered hateful or highly offensive
X. Something of little importance or value
Y. Cause of harm, ruin, or death

The Lion, The Witch & The Wardrobe Vocabulary Matching 3 Answer Key

W - 1.	VERMIN	A.	Frustrating; cursed
O - 2.	SATYR	B.	Kind of gate that controls the rate of water flow through a channel
Q - 3.	CENTAUR	C.	Elastic, soft, bouncy
K - 4.	PREMISES	D.	Moved as a group
B - 5.	SLUICE	E.	Tree branches, especially large or main branches
H - 6.	RENOUNCED	F.	Small tower extending above a building
Y - 7.	BANE	G.	High-pitched and piercing in tone or sound
J - 8.	GAIETY	H.	Given up, especially by formal announcement
U - 9.	SLEDGE	I.	Loose, sleeveless coat worn over outer garments; cloak
C - 10.	SPRINGY	J.	State of joyful exuberance or merriment
S - 11.	TOKEN	K.	A building and its surrounding grounds
L - 12.	PARCELS	L.	Packages; wrapped-up items
V - 13.	PRODIGIOUS	M.	Place, such as a pantry or cellar, where food is stored
D - 14.	TROOPED	N.	Kind of tree with clusters of yellow flowers
G - 15.	SHRILL	O.	Mythological creature composed of part man and part goat
N - 16.	LABURNUM	P.	Gracefully slender; moving and blending with ease
I - 17.	MANTLE	Q.	Mythical being that is half man and half horse
E - 18.	BOUGHS	R.	A disrespectful laugh
M - 19.	LARDER	S.	Something serving as proof of something else; a sign
P - 20.	LITHE	T.	Pouting and withdrawn
R - 21.	SNIGGER	U.	Vehicle mounted on runners, drawn by work animals across ice
A - 22.	DRATTED	V.	Impressively great in size or force
F - 23.	TURRET	W.	Pests; people considered hateful or highly offensive
X - 24.	TRIFLE	X.	Something of little importance or value
T - 25.	SULKY	Y.	Cause of harm, ruin, or death

The Lion, The Witch & The Wardrobe Vocabulary Matching 4

___ 1. SOLEMN   A. Tree branches, especially large or main branches
___ 2. PEDLARS   B. Verbal abuse; taunting
___ 3. CAMPAIGN   C. With warmth and sincerity
___ 4. SHRILL   D. Not to be relied on; not dependable or trustworthy; dangerous
___ 5. FESTOONS   E. Mythological creature composed of part man and part goat
___ 6. TROOPED   F. An act intended to deceive or trick
___ 7. SPRINGY   G. Something used to lure victims into danger
___ 8. PROPHECY   H. Prediction of the future
___ 9. BOUGHS   I. Signaled or summoned, as by nodding or waving
___10. PARCELS   J. Influenced by charms or spells
___11. REMNANTS   K. Pests; people considered hateful or highly offensive
___12. JEERING   L. Moved as a group
___13. BECKONED   M. Deeply earnest, serious, and sober
___14. CENTAUR   N. Left-overs
___15. ENCHANTED   O. Elastic, soft, bouncy
___16. GIBBER   P. British word for one who travels about selling wares
___17. HOAX   Q. High-pitched and piercing in tone or sound
___18. VERMIN   R. Offensive or disgusting
___19. DECOY   S. Packages; wrapped-up items
___20. WRETCHED   T. Mythical being that is half man and half horse
___21. HEARTILY   U. Rapidly speak about unimportant matters
___22. MUFFLER   V. Heavy scarf worn around the neck for warmth
___23. SATYR   W. Military operation or plan
___24. REPULSIVE   X. Decorative garlands of flowers or leaves
___25. TREACHEROUS   Y. Of a poor or mean character

The Lion, The Witch & The Wardrobe Vocabulary Matching 4 Answer Key

M - 1.	SOLEMN	A. Tree branches, especially large or main branches
P - 2.	PEDLARS	B. Verbal abuse; taunting
W - 3.	CAMPAIGN	C. With warmth and sincerity
Q - 4.	SHRILL	D. Not to be relied on; not dependable or trustworthy; dangerous
X - 5.	FESTOONS	E. Mythological creature composed of part man and part goat
L - 6.	TROOPED	F. An act intended to deceive or trick
O - 7.	SPRINGY	G. Something used to lure victims into danger
H - 8.	PROPHECY	H. Prediction of the future
A - 9.	BOUGHS	I. Signaled or summoned, as by nodding or waving
S - 10.	PARCELS	J. Influenced by charms or spells
N - 11.	REMNANTS	K. Pests; people considered hateful or highly offensive
B - 12.	JEERING	L. Moved as a group
I - 13.	BECKONED	M. Deeply earnest, serious, and sober
T - 14.	CENTAUR	N. Left-overs
J - 15.	ENCHANTED	O. Elastic, soft, bouncy
U - 16.	GIBBER	P. British word for one who travels about selling wares
F - 17.	HOAX	Q. High-pitched and piercing in tone or sound
K - 18.	VERMIN	R. Offensive or disgusting
G - 19.	DECOY	S. Packages; wrapped-up items
Y - 20.	WRETCHED	T. Mythical being that is half man and half horse
C - 21.	HEARTILY	U. Rapidly speak about unimportant matters
V - 22.	MUFFLER	V. Heavy scarf worn around the neck for warmth
E - 23.	SATYR	W. Military operation or plan
R - 24.	REPULSIVE	X. Decorative garlands of flowers or leaves
D - 25.	TREACHEROUS	Y. Of a poor or mean character

The Lion, The Witch & The Wardrobe Vocabulary Magic Squares 1

Match the definition with the vocabulary word. Put your answers in the magic squares below. When your answers are correct, all columns and rows will add to the same number.

A. JOLLIFICATION
B. SHORN
C. MANTLE
D. WRETCHED
E. LITHE
F. BANE
G. PREMISES
H. GIBBER
I. PAVILION
J. DIN
K. LARDER
L. LULLING
M. LEERING
N. RABBLE
O. RESUMED
P. ALLIANCE

1. Cause of harm, ruin, or death
2. Ornate tent
3. Began again; continued after interruption
4. Of a poor or mean character
5. Look with a sidelong glance with evil intent
6. Shaved
7. Rapidly speak about unimportant matters
8. Place, such as a pantry or cellar, where food is stored
9. Loose, sleeveless coat worn over outer garments; cloak
10. Political partnership
11. Loud, harsh noise
12. Gracefully slender; moving and blending with ease
13. Soothing; calming; causing to sleep or rest
14. A building and its surrounding grounds
15. Festivity; revelry
16. Disorderly crowd of people

A=	B=	C=	D=
E=	F=	G=	H=
I=	J=	K=	L=
M=	N=	O=	P=

The Lion, The Witch & The Wardrobe Vocabulary Magic Squares 1 Answer Key

Match the definition with the vocabulary word. Put your answers in the magic squares below. When your answers are correct, all columns and rows will add to the same number.

A. JOLLIFICATION
B. SHORN
C. MANTLE
D. WRETCHED
E. LITHE
F. BANE
G. PREMISES
H. GIBBER
I. PAVILION
J. DIN
K. LARDER
L. LULLING
M. LEERING
N. RABBLE
O. RESUMED
P. ALLIANCE

1. Cause of harm, ruin, or death
2. Ornate tent
3. Began again; continued after interruption
4. Of a poor or mean character
5. Look with a sidelong glance with evil intent
6. Shaved
7. Rapidly speak about unimportant matters
8. Place, such as a pantry or cellar, where food is stored
9. Loose, sleeveless coat worn over outer garments; cloak
10. Political partnership
11. Loud, harsh noise
12. Gracefully slender; moving and blending with ease
13. Soothing; calming; causing to sleep or rest
14. A building and its surrounding grounds
15. Festivity; revelry
16. Disorderly crowd of people

A=15	B=6	C=9	D=4
E=12	F=1	G=14	H=7
I=2	J=11	K=8	L=13
M=5	N=16	O=3	P=10

The Lion, The Witch & The Wardrobe Vocabulary Magic Squares 2

Match the definition with the vocabulary word. Put your answers in the magic squares below. When your answers are correct, all columns and rows will add to the same number.

A. STRATAGEM
B. LABURNUM
C. BANE
D. WHET

E. CENTAUR
F. BOUGHS
G. RABBLE
H. HOAX

I. TOKEN
J. ALIGHTING
K. LULLING
L. MANTLE

M. DISPOSAL
N. HEARTILY
O. GLUTTONY
P. BECKONED

1. An act intended to deceive or trick
2. Military plan designed to deceive or surprise an enemy
3. Kind of tree with clusters of yellow flowers
4. Disorderly crowd of people
5. Coming down and settling, as after flight
6. Excess in eating or drinking
7. Signaled or summoned, as by nodding or waving
8. Something serving as proof of something else; a sign
9. Soothing; calming; causing to sleep or rest
10. With warmth and sincerity
11. To allow one to use or be of service to another
12. Loose, sleeveless coat worn over outer garments; cloak
13. Mythical being that is half man and half horse
14. Sharpen
15. Cause of harm, ruin, or death
16. Tree branches, especially large or main branches

A=	B=	C=	D=
E=	F=	G=	H=
I=	J=	K=	L=
M=	N=	O=	P=

The Lion, The Witch & The Wardrobe Vocabulary Magic Squares 2 Answer Key

Match the definition with the vocabulary word. Put your answers in the magic squares below. When your answers are correct, all columns and rows will add to the same number.

A. STRATAGEM
B. LABURNUM
C. BANE
D. WHET

E. CENTAUR
F. BOUGHS
G. RABBLE
H. HOAX

I. TOKEN
J. ALIGHTING
K. LULLING
L. MANTLE

M. DISPOSAL
N. HEARTILY
O. GLUTTONY
P. BECKONED

1. An act intended to deceive or trick
2. Military plan designed to deceive or surprise an enemy
3. Kind of tree with clusters of yellow flowers
4. Disorderly crowd of people
5. Coming down and settling, as after flight
6. Excess in eating or drinking
7. Signaled or summoned, as by nodding or waving
8. Something serving as proof of something else; a sign
9. Soothing; calming; causing to sleep or rest
10. With warmth and sincerity
11. To allow one to use or be of service to another
12. Loose, sleeveless coat worn over outer garments; cloak
13. Mythical being that is half man and half horse
14. Sharpen
15. Cause of harm, ruin, or death
16. Tree branches, especially large or main branches

A=2	B=3	C=15	D=14
E=13	F=16	G=4	H=1
I=8	J=5	K=9	L=12
M=11	N=10	O=6	P=7

The Lion, The Witch & The Wardrobe Vocabulary Magic Squares 3

Match the definition with the vocabulary word. Put your answers in the magic squares below. When your answers are correct, all columns and rows will add to the same number.

A. MUFFLER
B. REPULSIVE
C. RECKONED
D. INQUISITIVE
E. SATYR
F. BOUGHS
G. VERMIN
H. SHORN
I. DIN
J. MANTLE
K. INCANTATION
L. SPRINGY
M. BRISTLING
N. FRATERNIZING
O. JOLLIFICATION
P. GLADE

1. Heavy scarf worn around the neck for warmth
2. Associating with others in a brotherly way
3. Loose, sleeveless coat worn over outer garments; cloak
4. Mythological creature composed of part man and part goat
5. Pests; people considered hateful or highly offensive
6. Elastic, soft, bouncy
7. Open space in a forest
8. Relied on with confidence
9. Festivity; revelry
10. Inclined to investigate; eager for knowledge
11. Shaved
12. Words believed to have a magical effect; a spell
13. Loud, harsh noise
14. Tree branches, especially large or main branches
15. Offensive or disgusting
16. Standing stiffly on end

A=	B=	C=	D=
E=	F=	G=	H=
I=	J=	K=	L=
M=	N=	O=	P=

The Lion, The Witch & The Wardrobe Vocabulary Magic Squares 3 Answer Key

Match the definition with the vocabulary word. Put your answers in the magic squares below. When your answers are correct, all columns and rows will add to the same number.

A. MUFFLER
B. REPULSIVE
C. RECKONED
D. INQUISITIVE
E. SATYR
F. BOUGHS
G. VERMIN
H. SHORN
I. DIN
J. MANTLE
K. INCANTATION
L. SPRINGY
M. BRISTLING
N. FRATERNIZING
O. JOLLIFICATION
P. GLADE

1. Heavy scarf worn around the neck for warmth
2. Associating with others in a brotherly way
3. Loose, sleeveless coat worn over outer garments; cloak
4. Mythological creature composed of part man and part goat
5. Pests; people considered hateful or highly offensive
6. Elastic, soft, bouncy
7. Open space in a forest
8. Relied on with confidence
9. Festivity; revelry
10. Inclined to investigate; eager for knowledge
11. Shaved
12. Words believed to have a magical effect; a spell
13. Loud, harsh noise
14. Tree branches, especially large or main branches
15. Offensive or disgusting
16. Standing stiffly on end

A=1	B=15	C=8	D=10
E=4	F=14	G=5	H=11
I=13	J=3	K=12	L=6
M=16	N=2	O=9	P=7

The Lion, The Witch & The Wardrobe Vocabulary Magic Squares 4

Match the definition with the vocabulary word. Put your answers in the magic squares below. When your answers are correct, all columns and rows will add to the same number.

A. SHRILL
B. ABIDE
C. CENTAUR
D. REMNANTS
E. INCANTATION
F. SHORN
G. MELANCHOLY
H. FOREBODING
I. BEASTLY
J. PAVILION
K. SLEDGE
L. CAMPAIGN
M. FRATERNIZING
N. BOUGHS
O. RECKONED
P. SLUICE

1. Sense of impending evil or misfortune
2. Associating with others in a brotherly way
3. Put up with; tolerate
4. Vehicle mounted on runners, drawn by work animals across ice
5. Ornate tent
6. Mythical being that is half man and half horse
7. Kind of gate that controls the rate of water flow through a channel
8. Words believed to have a magical effect; a spell
9. Relied on with confidence
10. Shaved
11. Very disagreeable; unpleasant
12. Left-overs
13. High-pitched and piercing in tone or sound
14. Military operation or plan
15. Sadness or depression of the spirits
16. Tree branches, especially large or main branches

A=	B=	C=	D=
E=	F=	G=	H=
I=	J=	K=	L=
M=	N=	O=	P=

The Lion, The Witch & The Wardrobe Vocabulary Magic Squares 4 Answer Key

Match the definition with the vocabulary word. Put your answers in the magic squares below. When your answers are correct, all columns and rows will add to the same number.

A. SHRILL   E. INCANTATION   I. BEASTLY   M. FRATERNIZING
B. ABIDE   F. SHORN   J. PAVILION   N. BOUGHS
C. CENTAUR   G. MELANCHOLY   K. SLEDGE   O. RECKONED
D. REMNANTS   H. FOREBODING   L. CAMPAIGN   P. SLUICE

1. Sense of impending evil or misfortune
2. Associating with others in a brotherly way
3. Put up with; tolerate
4. Vehicle mounted on runners, drawn by work animals across ice
5. Ornate tent
6. Mythical being that is half man and half horse
7. Kind of gate that controls the rate of water flow through a channel
8. Words believed to have a magical effect; a spell
9. Relied on with confidence
10. Shaved
11. Very disagreeable; unpleasant
12. Left-overs
13. High-pitched and piercing in tone or sound
14. Military operation or plan
15. Sadness or depression of the spirits
16. Tree branches, especially large or main branches

A=13	B=3	C=6	D=12
E=8	F=10	G=15	H=1
I=11	J=5	K=4	L=14
M=2	N=16	O=9	P=7

Copyrighted

The Lion, The Witch & The Wardrobe Vocabulary Word Search 1

```
D R A T T E D M A N T L E P B O U G H S
T T L M Q N G Y S E S I M E R P S B N W
V Z L W G U C A M P H O R D B V S C M G
D W I M J P A V I L I O N L D H P R E J
B E A S T L Y R T L C R N A E C I U L S
X M N R Y G N I R P S P E R T D T C O C
F J C L D B S A T Y R R E S U M E D S G
S R E Q B R S W O M Y G U Q S N F E W T
T H A V A Y O C Z G Q O V R T U U N H B
A K O T N H E B N V R C P A X W L O E P
G R Q R E D W I E E E C U A J Y A K T R
B A J D N R D K H L L R O F R X R C Y T
T B I H T O N C F E F H M R P C D E K L
V B W O B U A I E T F C G I D L E B V R
A L K E S E R R Z N U H L D N I R L F Z
D E R H R T I R K I M Y A I K T A W S F
N O C T V N L L E C N X D N T H L L J Q
F C W E G D E L S T J G E Y T E I A G S
```

A building and its surrounding grounds (8)
An act intended to deceive or trick (4)
Associating with others in a brotherly way (12)
Began again; continued after interruption (7)
British word for one who travels about selling wares (7)
Cause of harm, ruin, or death (4)
Compound made of bark and leaves, used to repel insects (7)
Deeply earnest, serious, and sober (6)
Disorderly crowd of people (6)
Elastic, soft, bouncy (7)
Frustrating; cursed (7)
Gracefully slender; moving and blending with ease (5)
Heavy scarf worn around the neck for warmth (7)
Invigorating & stimulating tonic (7)
Kind of gate that controls the rate of water flow through a channel (6)
Look with a sidelong glance with evil intent (7)
Loose, sleeveless coat worn over outer garments; cloak (6)
Loud, harsh noise (3)
Mythical being that is half man and half horse (7)
Mythological creature composed of part man and part goat (5)
Not to be relied on; not dependable or trustworthy; dangerous (11)
Open space in a forest (5)
Ornate tent (8)

Packages; wrapped-up items (7)
Pests; people considered hateful or highly offensive (6)
Place, such as a pantry or cellar, where food is stored (6)
Political partnership (8)
Pouting and withdrawn (5)
Prey; a hunted animal (6)
Put up with; tolerate (5)
Sense of impending evil or misfortune (10)
Sharpen (4)
Shaved (5)
Showing ill will and a desire to hurt (8)
Signaled or summoned, as by nodding or waving (8)
Small tower extending above a building (6)
Something of little importance or value (6)
Something serving as proof of something else; a sign (5)
Something used to lure victims into danger (5)
State of joyful exuberance or merriment (6)
Structures that taper to a point at the top (6)
Tall cabinet or closet built to hold clothes (8)
The adult male of various deer (4)
Tree branches, especially large or main branches (6)
Vehicle mounted on runners, drawn by work animals across ice (6)
Very disagreeable; unpleasant (7)

The Lion, The Witch & The Wardrobe Vocabulary Word Search 1 Answer Key

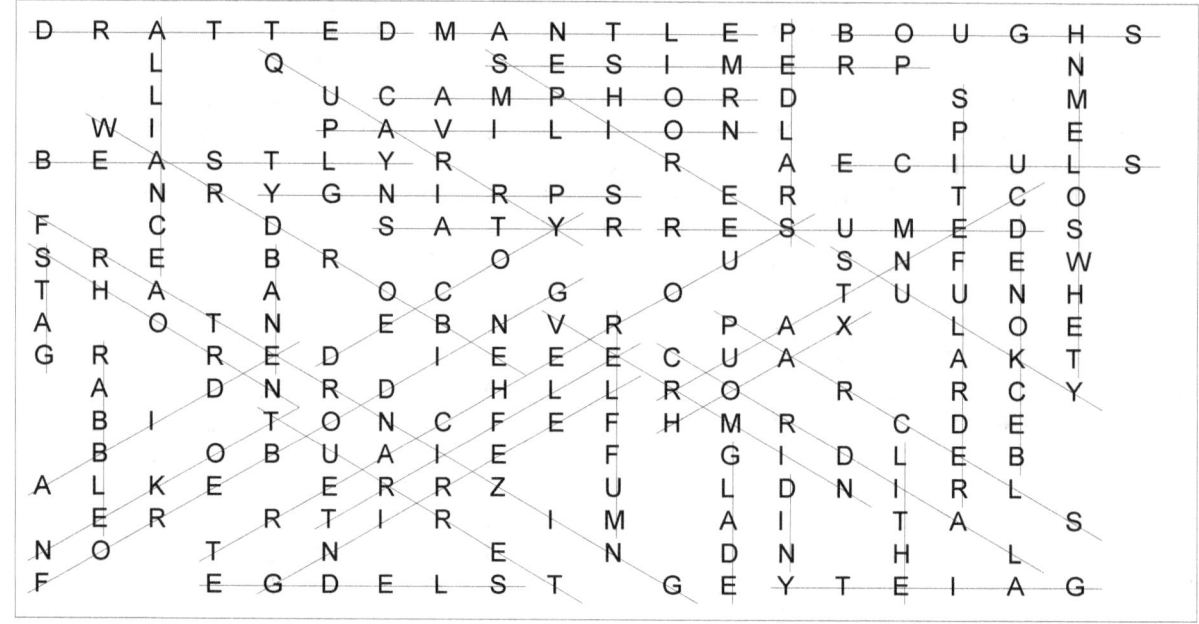

A building and its surrounding grounds (8)
An act intended to deceive or trick (4)
Associating with others in a brotherly way (12)
Began again; continued after interruption (7)
British word for one who travels about selling wares (7)
Cause of harm, ruin, or death (4)
Compound made of bark and leaves, used to repel insects (7)
Deeply earnest, serious, and sober (6)
Disorderly crowd of people (6)
Elastic, soft, bouncy (7)
Frustrating; cursed (7)
Gracefully slender; moving and blending with ease (5)
Heavy scarf worn around the neck for warmth (7)
Invigorating & stimulating tonic (7)
Kind of gate that controls the rate of water flow through a channel (6)
Look with a sidelong glance with evil intent (7)
Loose, sleeveless coat worn over outer garments; cloak (6)
Loud, harsh noise (3)
Mythical being that is half man and half horse (7)
Mythological creature composed of part man and part goat (5)
Not to be relied on; not dependable or trustworthy; dangerous (11)
Open space in a forest (5)
Ornate tent (8)

Packages; wrapped-up items (7)
Pests; people considered hateful or highly offensive (6)
Place, such as a pantry or cellar, where food is stored (6)
Political partnership (8)
Pouting and withdrawn (5)
Prey; a hunted animal (6)
Put up with; tolerate (5)
Sense of impending evil or misfortune (10)
Sharpen (4)
Shaved (5)
Showing ill will and a desire to hurt (8)
Signaled or summoned, as by nodding or waving (8)
Small tower extending above a building (6)
Something of little importance or value (6)
Something serving as proof of something else; a sign (5)
Something used to lure victims into danger (5)
State of joyful exuberance or merriment (6)
Structures that taper to a point at the top (6)
Tall cabinet or closet built to hold clothes (8)
The adult male of various deer (4)
Tree branches, especially large or main branches (6)
Vehicle mounted on runners, drawn by work animals across ice (6)
Very disagreeable; unpleasant (7)

The Lion, The Witch & The Wardrobe Vocabulary Word Search 2

```
B J S A Y B S H X C B N S O L E M N R P
R T P Q L M T L E S U E R J B D T B Y T
I P I Q W I A H Z A R K E E W J I A G P
S T R A T A G E M T R O H P M A C N S Q
T R E O T Z R H H Y I T T Y J N R E N M
L I S M P S W D T R N C I G N O A Y O G
I F U A M H L D R I G S L L H G G N O Y
N L M N E R E E H O N R M S Y N N C T G
G E E T R I M C F Q B G F E I I I W S S
G S D L E L J N Y O C E D R Y L R T E G
L N I E D L X U K K L A E R T L E Y F C
U I B H R V R O L S L E A X E U E R Q G
T G A X A E V N U G L N P Q I L J R D Z
T G M S L L J E S L I N G I A P M A C R
O E K F J V P R R D S L E D G E X U S Y
N R F Z W E K J R M R A B B L E J Q V B
Y U F V S T Z O E C I U L S H G U O B X
M P A V I L I O N Y G N I R P S H O A X
```

A buzzing or whirring sound (7)
A disrespectful laugh (7)
An act intended to deceive or trick (4)
Began again; continued after interruption (7)
Cause of harm, ruin, or death (4)
Coming down and settling, as after flight (9)
Compound made of bark and leaves, used to repel insects (7)
Cover over with a soft, furry covering (6)
Decorative garlands of flowers or leaves (8)
Deeply earnest, serious, and sober (6)
Disorderly crowd of people (6)
Elastic, soft, bouncy (7)
Excess in eating or drinking (8)
Given up, especially by formal announcement (9)
Gracefully slender; moving and blending with ease (5)
Heavy scarf worn around the neck for warmth (7)
High-pitched and piercing in tone or sound (6)
Kind of gate that controls the rate of water flow through a channel (6)
Left-overs (8)
Look with a sidelong glance with evil intent (7)
Loose, sleeveless coat worn over outer garments; cloak (6)
Loud, harsh noise (3)
Military operation or plan (8)
Military plan designed to deceive or surprise an enemy (9)
Mythological creature composed of part man and part goat (5)
Of no exceptional ability (8)
Open space in a forest (5)
Ornate tent (8)
Pests; people considered hateful or highly offensive (6)
Place, such as a pantry or cellar, where food is stored (6)
Pouting and withdrawn (5)
Prediction of the future (8)
Prey; a hunted animal (6)
Put up with; tolerate (5)
Sharpen (4)
Shaved (5)
Something of little importance or value (6)
Something serving as proof of something else; a sign (5)
Something used to lure victims into danger (5)
Soothing; calming; causing to sleep or rest (7)
Standing stiffly on end (9)
State of joyful exuberance or merriment (6)
Structures that taper to a point at the top (6)
Tall cabinet or closet built to hold clothes (8)
The adult male of various deer (4)
Tree branches, especially large or main branches (6)
Vehicle mounted on runners, drawn by work animals across ice (6)
Verbal abuse; taunting (7)
With warmth and sincerity (8)

The Lion, The Witch & The Wardrobe Vocabulary Word Search 2 Answer Key

```
B   S A     S H     B N S O L E M N
R   P I   T   E S U E R   D   B
I P I   W I A   A R K E E   I A
S T R A T A G E M T R O H P M A C N S
T R E O   R H   Y I T   N R E   N
L I S M P S W D T R N   O A   N O
I F U A H   D R I G   L H G G N O
N L M N E R E E   O N   S Y N   O T
G E E T R I   C   B G   E I I   S S
G S D L E L   N Y O C E D R Y L R   E
L N I E D L   U K   A E R T L E Y F
U I B   R V R O L   L E A   E U E R
T G A   A E V N U G L N   I L J R
O G   F L L   E S   I N G I A P M A C
N E   F   V   R R D S L E D G E   U
Y R   F   E   R M R A B B L E   Q
M P A V I L I O N Y G N I R P S H O A X
```

A buzzing or whirring sound (7)
A disrespectful laugh (7)
An act intended to deceive or trick (4)
Began again; continued after interruption (7)
Cause of harm, ruin, or death (4)
Coming down and settling, as after flight (9)
Compound made of bark and leaves, used to repel insects (7)
Cover over with a soft, furry covering (6)
Decorative garlands of flowers or leaves (8)
Deeply earnest, serious, and sober (6)
Disorderly crowd of people (6)
Elastic, soft, bouncy (7)
Excess in eating or drinking (8)
Given up, especially by formal announcement (9)
Gracefully slender; moving and blending with ease (5)
Heavy scarf worn around the neck for warmth (7)
High-pitched and piercing in tone or sound (6)
Kind of gate that controls the rate of water flow through a channel (6)
Left-overs (8)
Look with a sidelong glance with evil intent (7)
Loose, sleeveless coat worn over outer garments; cloak (6)
Loud, harsh noise (3)
Military operation or plan (8)
Military plan designed to deceive or surprise an enemy (9)
Mythological creature composed of part man and part goat (5)
Of no exceptional ability (8)
Open space in a forest (5)
Ornate tent (8)
Pests; people considered hateful or highly offensive (6)
Place, such as a pantry or cellar, where food is stored (6)
Pouting and withdrawn (5)
Prediction of the future (8)
Prey; a hunted animal (6)
Put up with; tolerate (5)
Sharpen (4)
Shaved (5)
Something of little importance or value (6)
Something serving as proof of something else; a sign (5)
Something used to lure victims into danger (5)
Soothing; calming; causing to sleep or rest (7)
Standing stiffly on end (9)
State of joyful exuberance or merriment (6)
Structures that taper to a point at the top (6)
Tall cabinet or closet built to hold clothes (8)
The adult male of various deer (4)
Tree branches, especially large or main branches (6)
Vehicle mounted on runners, drawn by work animals across ice (6)
Verbal abuse; taunting (7)
With warmth and sincerity (8)

The Lion, The Witch & The Wardrobe Vocabulary Word Search 3

```
L A I D R O C Q C V E L V E T A J T V N
L U F T V E G C K E G W S D S B E S E Y
I T L C Z N M P P K N J T A T I E U N L
R L U L I F B N T E W T R L A D R L T X
H J A R I T D M A F D X A G G E I K U R
S S E R R N N U P N A L T U Q D N Y R W
Z E N I D E G F B O T Q A H R E G W E B
L F F I G E T F H E N S G R N H L S D Y
S L M D G D R L S J A G E W S C U P S G
E O E J B G F E H L N S M H T F I H P
B L R C R E R O I M R T Y P E E R G M
S F A E A L K R R A E Y L L R T E U Y
U R N P M Y V R N N R V I D Y W I S O M
O A C U P N U T C R G S T E O M P N B F
R T H L H B L H A Z N F H C C Y S E G T
E E O S O E A U P A I T E N E B C P P Y
H R L I R N Q K P R D J K U D K Y A R N
C N Y V T D X P Q Q O C F O O X T R E P
A I V E R M I N L A B U R N U M E C M V
E Z D N L S V N F A E K E E T B I E I B
R I N V H J K B N Y R D Z R B U A L S K
T N S L X Y C E H P O R P I L X G S E J
R G Y T O K E N Y R F S G S A T Y R S N
```

ABIDE	GIBBER	PROPHECY	SPRINGY
BANE	GLADE	QUARRY	STAG
BEASTLY	HOAX	REMNANTS	STRATAGEM
BECKONED	JEERING	RENOUNCED	SULKY
BOUGHS	LABURNUM	REPULSIVE	TOKEN
BURRING	LARDER	SATYR	TREACHEROUS
CAMPHOR	LEERING	SHORN	TRIFLE
CENTAUR	LITHE	SHRILL	TURRET
CORDIAL	LULLING	SLEDGE	VELVET
DECOY	MANTLE	SLUICE	VENTURED
DIN	MELANCHOLY	SNAPPISHLY	VERMIN
ENCHANTED	MUFFLER	SNIGGER	WHET
FOREBODING	PARCELS	SOLEMN	WRETCHED
FRATERNIZING	PEDLARS	SPIRES	
GAIETY	PREMISES	SPITEFUL	

The Lion, The Witch & The Wardrobe Vocabulary Word Search 3 Answer Key

ABIDE	GIBBER	PROPHECY	SPRINGY
BANE	GLADE	QUARRY	STAG
BEASTLY	HOAX	REMNANTS	STRATAGEM
BECKONED	JEERING	RENOUNCED	SULKY
BOUGHS	LABURNUM	REPULSIVE	TOKEN
BURRING	LARDER	SATYR	TREACHEROUS
CAMPHOR	LEERING	SHORN	TRIFLE
CENTAUR	LITHE	SHRILL	TURRET
CORDIAL	LULLING	SLEDGE	VELVET
DECOY	MANTLE	SLUICE	VENTURED
DIN	MELANCHOLY	SNAPPISHLY	VERMIN
ENCHANTED	MUFFLER	SNIGGER	WHET
FOREBODING	PARCELS	SOLEMN	WRETCHED
FRATERNIZING	PEDLARS	SPIRES	
GAIETY	PREMISES	SPITEFUL	

The Lion, The Witch & The Wardrobe Vocabulary Word Search 4

```
H Y W A R D R O B E S S J T N N E B S N
S T R A T A G E M V D O C O R D I A L V
J E B Z E Z H A M E B L B E A I T N I M
O I U B H H N C H N Y E J L N Y F E T Q
L A R Z W T Z C T T A M G Z R T Z L H K
L G R Q L S T A G U Y N R E D R A L E R
I M I E W E N N D R O C T D S P L U Y L
F L N D R Y I I P E C P G S U Q L B R J
I C G W I R L R G D E A E J L P I O V K
C T O K E N E D G D E L S K R A U E L
A U V E A B E S I G E D B I Y O N G R V
T R J G B B R H U S P R B H G P C H M Q
I R C I Q E I K B M P D A O N H E S I G
O E G M C S N D H R E O R A F E T K N D
N T T I E V G N E N D D S X H C N I E Z
V R U R X N H L O G L S C A F Y L T N Q
L L I R H S F K Z K A H W M L L T G Q G
S P N J D F C X B N R O C Q U A R R Y H
S L G K U E M V P N S R T L R K J N P D
J X V M R V E L V E T N Q D E P O O R T
```

ABIDE	GIBBER	QUARRY	STAG
ALIGHTING	GLADE	RABBLE	STRATAGEM
ALLIANCE	HOAX	RECKONED	SULKY
BANE	JEERING	REMNANTS	TOKEN
BOUGHS	JOLLIFICATION	RESUMED	TRIFLE
BURRING	LARDER	SATYR	TROOPED
CENTAUR	LEERING	SHORN	TURRET
CORDIAL	LITHE	SHRILL	VELVET
DECOY	LULLING	SLEDGE	VENTURED
DIN	MANTLE	SLUICE	VERMIN
DISPOSAL	MUFFLER	SNIGGER	WARDROBE
DRATTED	PEDLARS	SOLEMN	WHET
GAIETY	PROPHECY	SPIRES	WRETCHED

The Lion, The Witch & The Wardrobe Vocabulary Word Search 4 Answer Key

ABIDE	GIBBER	QUARRY	STAG
ALIGHTING	GLADE	RABBLE	STRATAGEM
ALLIANCE	HOAX	RECKONED	SULKY
BANE	JEERING	REMNANTS	TOKEN
BOUGHS	JOLLIFICATION	RESUMED	TRIFLE
BURRING	LARDER	SATYR	TROOPED
CENTAUR	LEERING	SHORN	TURRET
CORDIAL	LITHE	SHRILL	VELVET
DECOY	LULLING	SLEDGE	VENTURED
DIN	MANTLE	SLUICE	VERMIN
DISPOSAL	MUFFLER	SNIGGER	WARDROBE
DRATTED	PEDLARS	SOLEMN	WHET
GAIETY	PROPHECY	SPIRES	WRETCHED

The Lion, The Witch & The Wardrobe Vocabulary Crossword 1

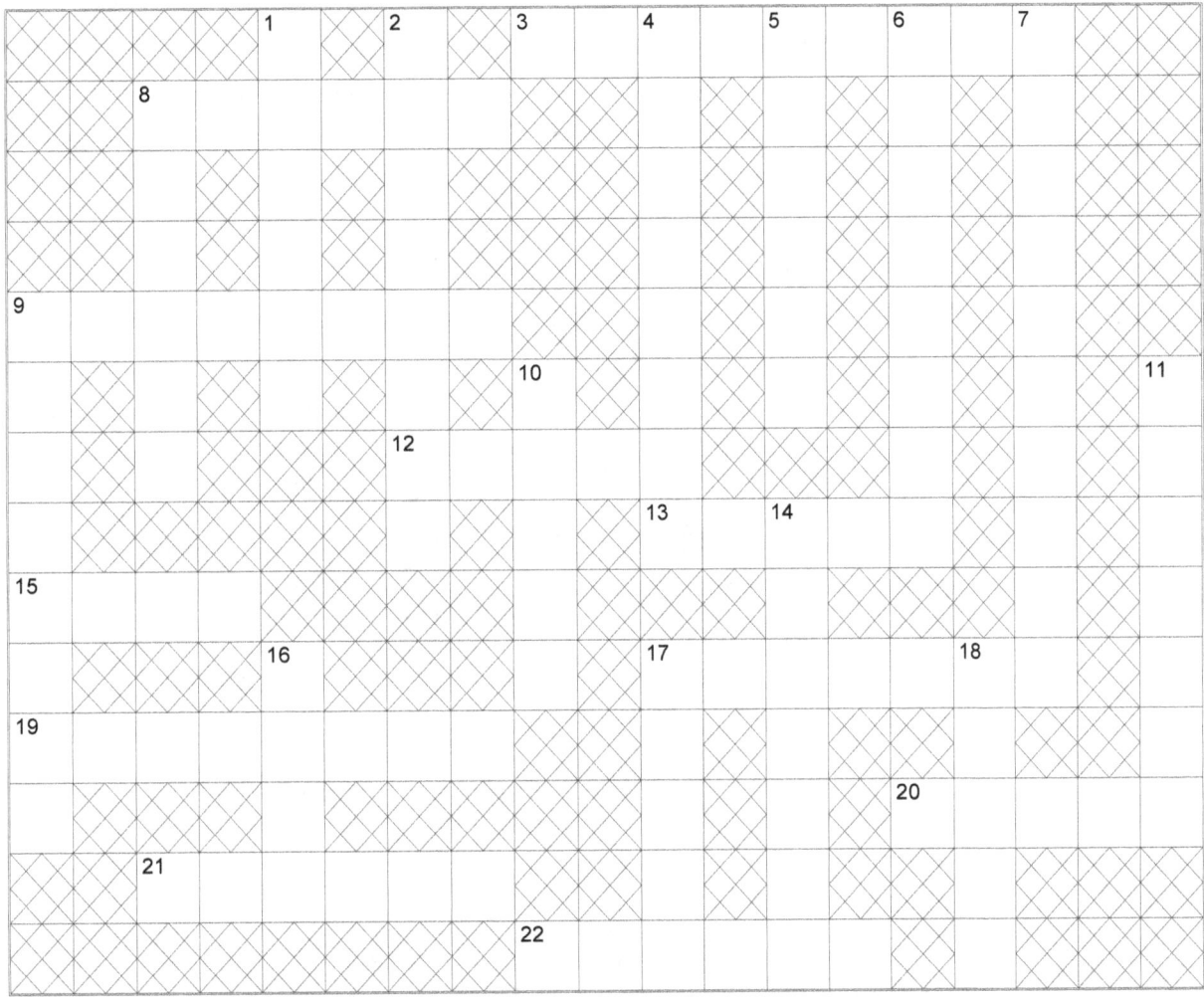

Across
3. Military plan designed to deceive or surprise an enemy
8. Pests; people considered hateful or highly offensive
9. Ornate tent
12. Put up with; tolerate
13. Something used to lure victims into danger
15. An act intended to deceive or trick
17. Elastic, soft, bouncy
19. Military operation or plan
20. Mythological creature composed of part man and part goat
21. Vehicle mounted on runners, drawn by work animals across ice
22. Loose, sleeveless coat worn over outer garments; cloak

Down
1. Something of little importance or value
2. To allow one to use or be of service to another
4. Relied on with confidence
5. Small tower extending above a building
6. Excess in eating or drinking
7. Sadness or depression of the spirits
8. Cover over with a soft, furry covering
9. Prediction of the future
10. Gracefully slender; moving and blending with ease
11. A disrespectful laugh
14. Invigorating & stimulating tonic
16. Cause of harm, ruin, or death
17. Shaved
18. Open space in a forest

The Lion, The Witch & The Wardrobe Vocabulary Crossword 1 Answer Key

			1 T		2 D		3 S	T	4 R	5 A	T	6 A	G	E	M	
		8 V	E	R	M	I	N		E		U		L		E	
			E		I		S		C		R		U		L	
			L		F		P		K		R		T		A	
9 P	A	V	I	L	I	O	N		O		E		T		N	
R	E		E		S		10 L		N		T		O		C	11 S
O		T			12 A	B	I	D	E				N		H	N
P					L		T		13 D	14 E	C	O	Y		O	I
15 H	O	A	X				H			O					L	G
E			16 B				E		17 S	P	R	I	18 N	G	Y	G
19 C	A	M	P	A	I	G	N		H		D		L			E
Y			N						O		I		20 S	A	T	Y	R
		21 S	L	E	D	G	E		R		A		D			
							22 M	A	N	T	L	E		E		

Across
3. Military plan designed to deceive or surprise an enemy
8. Pests; people considered hateful or highly offensive
9. Ornate tent
12. Put up with; tolerate
13. Something used to lure victims into danger
15. An act intended to deceive or trick
17. Elastic, soft, bouncy
19. Military operation or plan
20. Mythological creature composed of part man and part goat
21. Vehicle mounted on runners, drawn by work animals across ice
22. Loose, sleeveless coat worn over outer garments; cloak

Down
1. Something of little importance or value
2. To allow one to use or be of service to another
4. Relied on with confidence
5. Small tower extending above a building
6. Excess in eating or drinking
7. Sadness or depression of the spirits
8. Cover over with a soft, furry covering
9. Prediction of the future
10. Gracefully slender; moving and blending with ease
11. A disrespectful laugh
14. Invigorating & stimulating tonic
16. Cause of harm, ruin, or death
17. Shaved
18. Open space in a forest

The Lion, The Witch & The Wardrobe Vocabulary Crossword 2

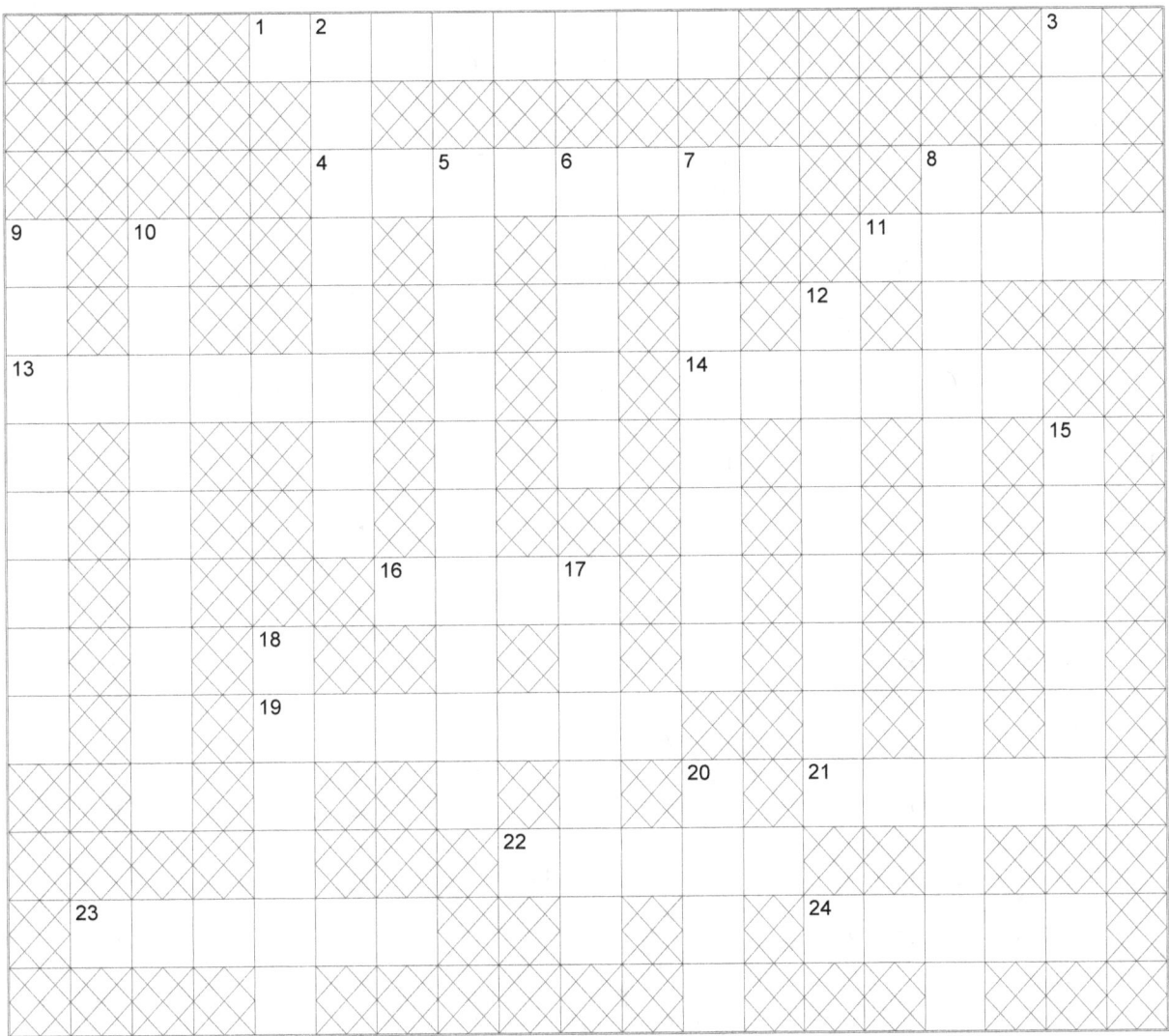

Across
1. Prediction of the future
4. Military operation or plan
11. Something serving as proof of something else; a sign
13. Pests; people considered hateful or highly offensive
14. Something of little importance or value
16. Sharpen
19. British word for one who travels about selling wares
21. Gracefully slender; moving and blending with ease
22. Something used to lure victims into danger
23. Deeply earnest, serious, and sober
24. Shaved

Down
2. Relied on with confidence
3. Cause of harm, ruin, or death
5. Sadness or depression of the spirits
6. Put up with; tolerate
7. Excess in eating or drinking
8. Festivity; revelry
9. Ornate tent
10. Military plan designed to deceive or surprise an enemy
12. To allow one to use or be of service to another
15. Vehicle mounted on runners, drawn by work animals across ice
17. Small tower extending above a building
18. Structures that taper to a point at the top
20. An act intended to deceive or trick

The Lion, The Witch & The Wardrobe Vocabulary Crossword 2 Answer Key

			1 P	2 R	O	P	H	E	C	Y			3 B	
				E									A	
			4 C	A	5 M	P	6 A	I	7 G	N		8 J	N	
9 P		10 S		K		E		B		L		11 T	O	K	E	N
A		T				O		L		I		12 D	L	
13 V	E	R	M	I	N	A	N	D	E	T	R	I	F	L	E	
I		A				E		N		E		T	S		I	15 S
L		T				D		C				O		P		F	L
I		A					16 W	H	E	17 T		N		O		I	E
O		G		18 S				O		U		Y		S		C	D
N		E		19 P	E	D	L	A	R	S				A		A	G
		M		I				Y		R		20 H		21 L	I	T	H	E
				R					22 D	E	C	O	Y		I	
		23 S	O	L	E	M	N			T		A		24 S	H	O	R	N
				S								X			N	

Across
1. Prediction of the future
4. Military operation or plan
11. Something serving as proof of something else; a sign
13. Pests; people considered hateful or highly offensive
14. Something of little importance or value
16. Sharpen
19. British word for one who travels about selling wares
21. Gracefully slender; moving and blending with ease
22. Something used to lure victims into danger
23. Deeply earnest, serious, and sober
24. Shaved

Down
2. Relied on with confidence
3. Cause of harm, ruin, or death
5. Sadness or depression of the spirits
6. Put up with; tolerate
7. Excess in eating or drinking
8. Festivity; revelry
9. Ornate tent
10. Military plan designed to deceive or surprise an enemy
12. To allow one to use or be of service to another
15. Vehicle mounted on runners, drawn by work animals across ice
17. Small tower extending above a building
18. Structures that taper to a point at the top
20. An act intended to deceive or trick

The Lion, The Witch & The Wardrobe Vocabulary Crossword 3

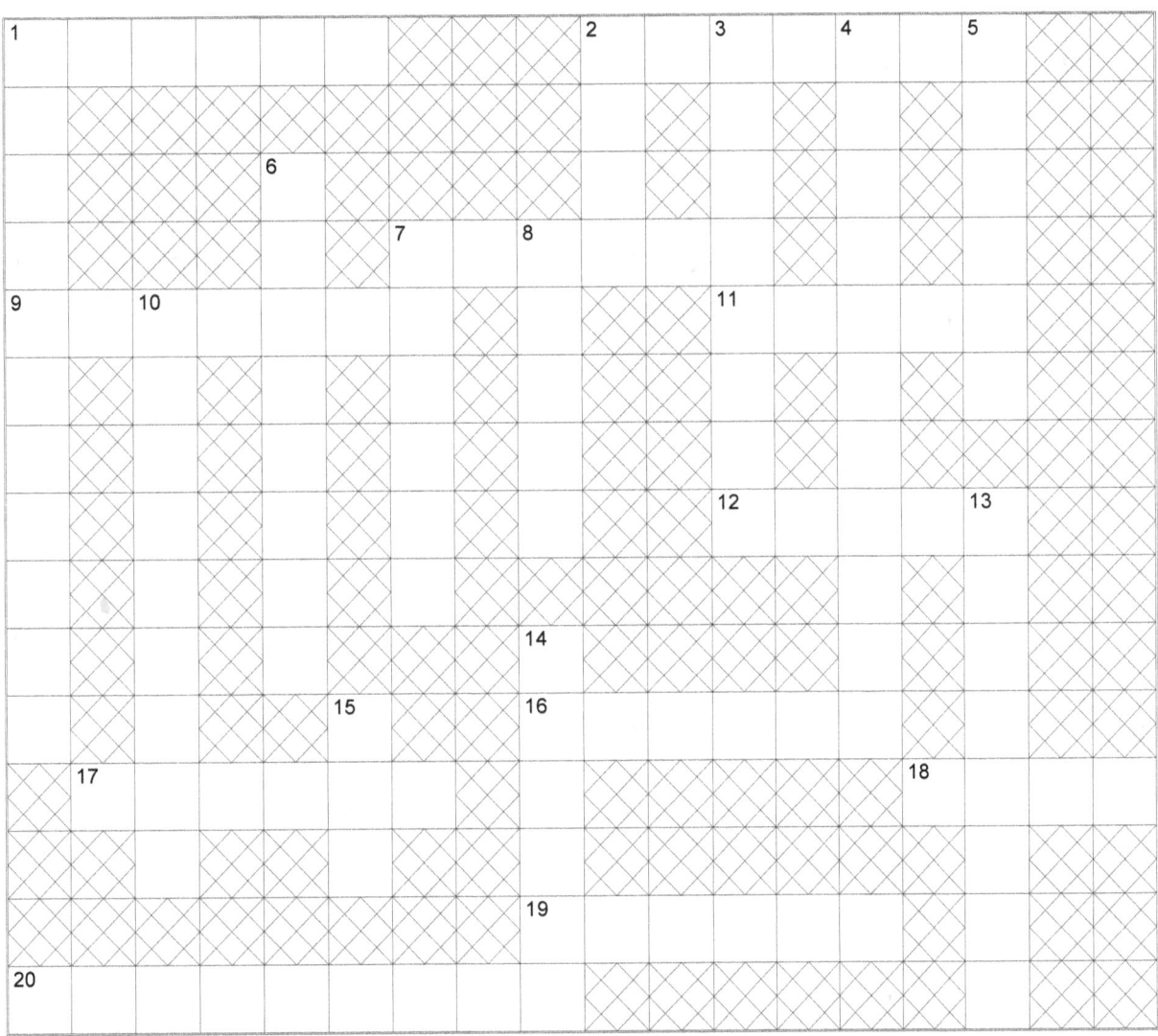

Across
1. Small tower extending above a building
2. A buzzing or whirring sound
7. Deeply earnest, serious, and sober
9. Invigorating & stimulating tonic
11. Put up with; tolerate
12. Mythological creature composed of part man and part goat
16. Disorderly crowd of people
17. Pests; people considered hateful or highly offensive
18. An act intended to deceive or trick
19. Place, such as a pantry or cellar, where food is stored
20. Offensive or disgusting

Down
1. Not to be relied on; not dependable or trustworthy; dangerous
2. Cause of harm, ruin, or death
3. Left-overs
4. Inclined to investigate; eager for knowledge
5. Rapidly speak about unimportant matters
6. Showing ill will and a desire to hurt
7. Vehicle mounted on runners, drawn by work animals across ice
8. Gracefully slender; moving and blending with ease
10. Given up, especially by formal announcement
13. Relied on with confidence
14. Something of little importance or value
15. Loud, harsh noise

The Lion, The Witch & The Wardrobe Vocabulary Crossword 3 Answer Key

	1 T	U	R	R	E	T		2 B	3 U	R	4 R	I	N	5 G	
	R							A		E		N		I	
	E				6 S			N		M		Q		B	
	A				P		7 S	8 O	L	E	M	N		U		B
9 C	O	10 R	D	I	A	L		I			11 A	B	I	D	E
	H		E		T			E			N		S		R
	E		N		E			D			T		I		
											12 S	A	T	Y	13 R
	R		O		F			G		E					E
	O		U		U			E					I		E
	U		N		L			14 T				V		C
	S		C		15 D		16 R	A	B	B	L	E		K
		17 V	E	R	M	I	N		I				18 H	O	A	X
			D			N				F				N	
								19 L	A	R	D	E	R		E
20 R	E	P	U	L	S	I	V	E						D	

Across
1. Small tower extending above a building
2. A buzzing or whirring sound
7. Deeply earnest, serious, and sober
9. Invigorating & stimulating tonic
11. Put up with; tolerate
12. Mythological creature composed of part man and part goat
16. Disorderly crowd of people
17. Pests; people considered hateful or highly offensive
18. An act intended to deceive or trick
19. Place, such as a pantry or cellar, where food is stored
20. Offensive or disgusting

Down
1. Not to be relied on; not dependable or trustworthy; dangerous
2. Cause of harm, ruin, or death
3. Left-overs
4. Inclined to investigate; eager for knowledge
5. Rapidly speak about unimportant matters
6. Showing ill will and a desire to hurt
7. Vehicle mounted on runners, drawn by work animals across ice
8. Gracefully slender; moving and blending with ease
10. Given up, especially by formal announcement
13. Relied on with confidence
14. Something of little importance or value
15. Loud, harsh noise

The Lion, The Witch & The Wardrobe Vocabulary Crossword 4

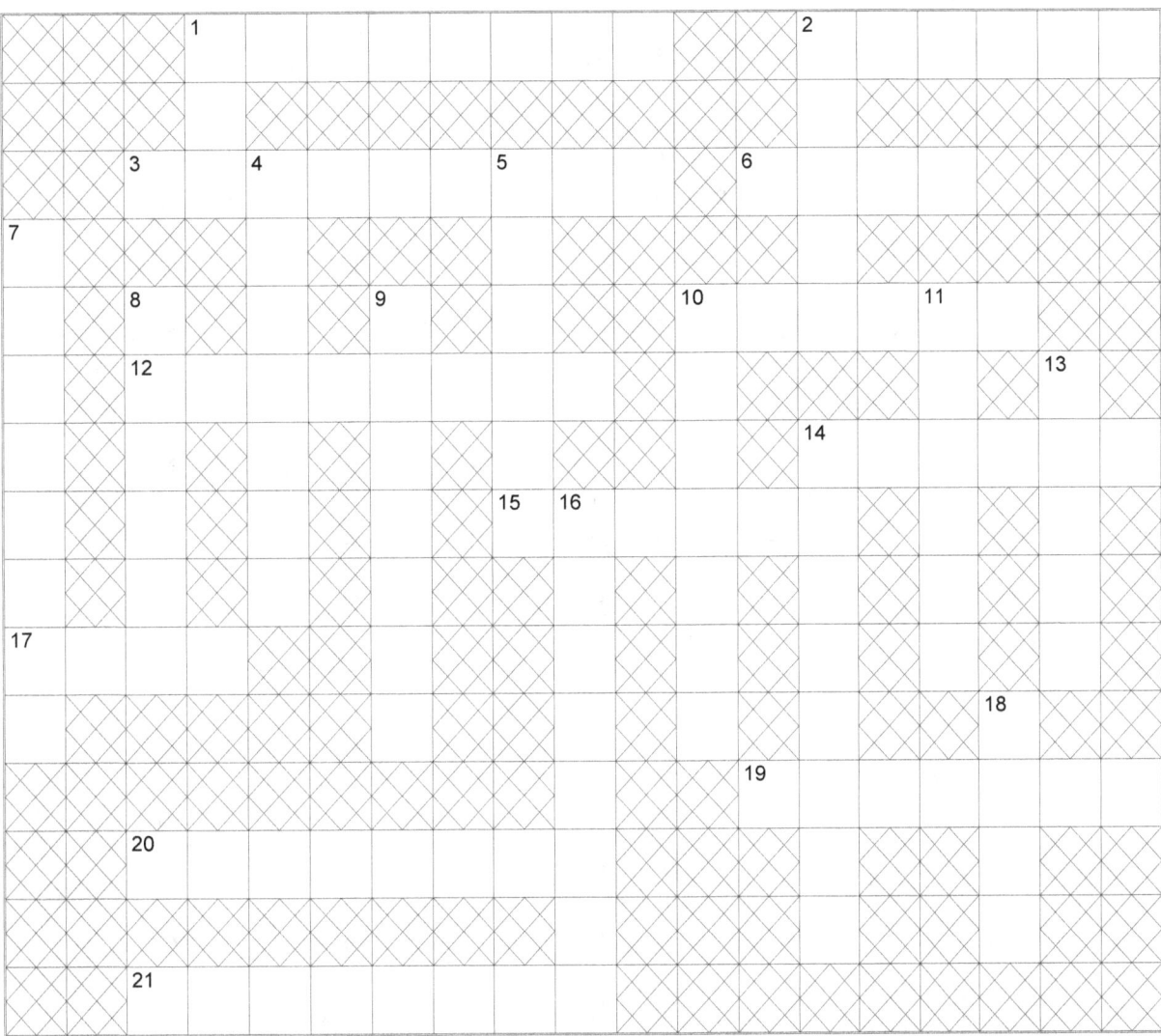

Across
1. To allow one to use or be of service to another
2. Vehicle mounted on runners, drawn by work animals across ice
3. Influenced by charms or spells
6. An act intended to deceive or trick
10. Loose, sleeveless coat worn over outer garments; cloak
12. Of no exceptional ability
14. Pests; people considered hateful or highly offensive
15. Something of little importance or value
17. Cause of harm, ruin, or death
19. Frustrating; cursed
20. Ornate tent
21. Of a poor or mean character

Down
1. Loud, harsh noise
2. Shaved
4. Invigorating & stimulating tonic
5. Small tower extending above a building
7. Tall cabinet or closet built to hold clothes
8. Deeply earnest, serious, and sober
9. A disrespectful laugh
10. Heavy scarf worn around the neck for warmth
11. Place, such as a pantry or cellar, where food is stored
13. Gracefully slender; moving and blending with ease
14. Took a risk; dared
16. Relied on with confidence
18. The adult male of various deer

The Lion, The Witch & The Wardrobe Vocabulary Crossword 4 Answer Key

			¹D	I	S	P	O	S	A	L		²S	L	E	D	G	E
			I									H					
		³E		⁴N	C	⁵H	A	N	T	E	⁶D		⁶H	O	A	X	
⁷W				O		U					R						
A		⁸S		R		⁹S		R		¹⁰M	A	N	T	¹¹L	E		
R		¹²O	R	D	I	N	A	R	Y	U				A		¹³L	
D		L		I		I		E		F		¹⁴V	E	R	M	I	N
R		E		A		G		¹⁵T	¹⁶R	I	F	L	E	D		T	
O		M		L		G		E		L		N		E		H	
¹⁷B	A	N	E			E		C		E		T		R		E	
E						R		K		R		U		¹⁸S			
								O		¹⁹D	R	A	T	T	E	D	
		²⁰P	A	V	I	L	I	O	N			E		A			
								E				D		G			
		²¹W	R	E	T	C	H	E	D								

Across
1. To allow one to use or be of service to another
2. Vehicle mounted on runners, drawn by work animals across ice
3. Influenced by charms or spells
6. An act intended to deceive or trick
10. Loose, sleeveless coat worn over outer garments; cloak
12. Of no exceptional ability
14. Pests; people considered hateful or highly offensive
15. Something of little importance or value
17. Cause of harm, ruin, or death
19. Frustrating; cursed
20. Ornate tent
21. Of a poor or mean character

Down
1. Loud, harsh noise
2. Shaved
4. Invigorating & stimulating tonic
5. Small tower extending above a building
7. Tall cabinet or closet built to hold clothes
8. Deeply earnest, serious, and sober
9. A disrespectful laugh
10. Heavy scarf worn around the neck for warmth
11. Place, such as a pantry or cellar, where food is stored
13. Gracefully slender; moving and blending with ease
14. Took a risk; dared
16. Relied on with confidence
18. The adult male of various deer

The Lion, The Witch & The Wardrobe Vocabulary Juggle Letters 1

1. RLNISGTBI = 1. _____
   Standing stiffly on end

2. XAHO = 2. _____
   An act intended to deceive or trick

3. LTERIF = 3. _____
   Something of little importance or value

4. LIRSLH = 4. _____
   High-pitched and piercing in tone or sound

5. PROTEDO = 5. _____
   Moved as a group

6. KYLSU = 6. _____
   Pouting and withdrawn

7. NBAE = 7. _____
   Cause of harm, ruin, or death

8. RGDIOSUOIP = 8. _____
   Impressively great in size or force

9. TCIANIONANT = 9. _____
   Words believed to have a magical effect; a spell

10. FTULSIPE = 10. _____
    Showing ill will and a desire to hurt

11. CLAAELIN = 11. _____
    Political partnership

12. OSUHBG = 12. _____
    Tree branches, especially large or main branches

13. RGNYIPS = 13. _____
    Elastic, soft, bouncy

14. RAERDL = 14. _____
    Place, such as a pantry or cellar, where food is stored

15. ENEKCDOB = 15. _____
    Signaled or summoned, as by nodding or waving

16. AIPLOSSD = 16. _____
    To allow one to use or be of service to another

The Lion, The Witch & The Wardrobe Vocabulary Juggle Letters 1 Answer Key

1. RLNISGTBI = 1. BRISTLING
   Standing stiffly on end

2. XAHO = 2. HOAX
   An act intended to deceive or trick

3. LTERIF = 3. TRIFLE
   Something of little importance or value

4. LIRSLH = 4. SHRILL
   High-pitched and piercing in tone or sound

5. PROTEDO = 5. TROOPED
   Moved as a group

6. KYLSU = 6. SULKY
   Pouting and withdrawn

7. NBAE = 7. BANE
   Cause of harm, ruin, or death

8. RGDIOSUOIP = 8. PRODIGIOUS
   Impressively great in size or force

9. TCIANIONANT = 9. INCANTATION
   Words believed to have a magical effect; a spell

10. FTULSIPE =10. SPITEFUL
    Showing ill will and a desire to hurt

11. CLAAELIN =11. ALLIANCE
    Political partnership

12. OSUHBG =12. BOUGHS
    Tree branches, especially large or main branches

13. RGNYIPS =13. SPRINGY
    Elastic, soft, bouncy

14. RAERDL =14. LARDER
    Place, such as a pantry or cellar, where food is stored

15. ENEKCDOB =15. BECKONED
    Signaled or summoned, as by nodding or waving

16. AIPLOSSD =16. DISPOSAL
    To allow one to use or be of service to another

The Lion, The Witch & The Wardrobe Vocabulary Juggle Letters 2

1. DEMREUS = 1. _____
   Began again; continued after interruption

2. REHWDETC = 2. _____
   Of a poor or mean character

3. BLBARE = 3. _____
   Disorderly crowd of people

4. DUVNTERE = 4. _____
   Took a risk; dared

5. LGNOYTTU = 5. _____
   Excess in eating or drinking

6. RPSEIS = 6. _____
   Structures that taper to a point at the top

7. RLIEEGN = 7. _____
   Look with a sidelong glance with evil intent

8. EDKCNEOB = 8. _____
   Signaled or summoned, as by nodding or waving

9. EDFGORBONI = 9. _____
   Sense of impending evil or misfortune

10. EREUSPLIV =10. _____
    Offensive or disgusting

11. ETAMNL =11. _____
    Loose, sleeveless coat worn over outer garments; cloak

12. KNREOEDC =12. _____
    Relied on with confidence

13. NIBGURR =13. _____
    A buzzing or whirring sound

14. GNIJEER =14. _____
    Verbal abuse; taunting

15. GAMETASTR =15. _____
    Military plan designed to deceive or surprise an enemy

16. NIAGMAPC =16. _____
    Military operation or plan

The Lion, The Witch & The Wardrobe Vocabulary Juggle Letters 2 Answer Key

1. DEMREUS = 1. RESUMED
   Began again; continued after interruption
2. REHWDETC = 2. WRETCHED
   Of a poor or mean character
3. BLBARE = 3. RABBLE
   Disorderly crowd of people
4. DUVNTERE = 4. VENTURED
   Took a risk; dared
5. LGNOYTTU = 5. GLUTTONY
   Excess in eating or drinking
6. RPSEIS = 6. SPIRES
   Structures that taper to a point at the top
7. RLIEEGN = 7. LEERING
   Look with a sidelong glance with evil intent
8. EDKCNEOB = 8. BECKONED
   Signaled or summoned, as by nodding or waving
9. EDFGORBONI = 9. FOREBODING
   Sense of impending evil or misfortune
10. EREUSPLIV = 10. REPULSIVE
    Offensive or disgusting
11. ETAMNL = 11. MANTLE
    Loose, sleeveless coat worn over outer garments; cloak
12. KNREOEDC = 12. RECKONED
    Relied on with confidence
13. NIBGURR = 13. BURRING
    A buzzing or whirring sound
14. GNIJEER = 14. JEERING
    Verbal abuse; taunting
15. GAMETASTR = 15. STRATAGEM
    Military plan designed to deceive or surprise an enemy
16. NIAGMAPC = 16. CAMPAIGN
    Military operation or plan

The Lion, The Witch & The Wardrobe Vocabulary Juggle Letters 3

1. OTERPDO = 1. _____
   Moved as a group

2. OSIDRGPUIO = 2. _____
   Impressively great in size or force

3. MGAAPICN = 3. _____
   Military operation or plan

4. FRMELUF = 4. _____
   Heavy scarf worn around the neck for warmth

5. SRIPES = 5. _____
   Structures that taper to a point at the top

6. RQRYUA = 6. _____
   Prey; a hunted animal

7. HEWT = 7. _____
   Sharpen

8. ERLADR = 8. _____
   Place, such as a pantry or cellar, where food is stored

9. AENB = 9. _____
   Cause of harm, ruin, or death

10. ECRLPAS =10. _____
    Packages; wrapped-up items

11. UTTLONGY =11. _____
    Excess in eating or drinking

12. RMINEV =12. _____
    Pests; people considered hateful or highly offensive

13. ESTAGMRAT =13. _____
    Military plan designed to deceive or surprise an enemy

14. DLSGEE =14. _____
    Vehicle mounted on runners, drawn by work animals across ice

15. GINERSG =15. _____
    A disrespectful laugh

16. SALPSIOD =16. _____
    To allow one to use or be of service to another

The Lion, The Witch & The Wardrobe Vocabulary Juggle Letters 3 Answer Key

1. OTERPDO = 1. TROOPED
   Moved as a group

2. OSIDRGPUIO = 2. PRODIGIOUS
   Impressively great in size or force

3. MGAAPICN = 3. CAMPAIGN
   Military operation or plan

4. FRMELUF = 4. MUFFLER
   Heavy scarf worn around the neck for warmth

5. SRIPES = 5. SPIRES
   Structures that taper to a point at the top

6. RQRYUA = 6. QUARRY
   Prey; a hunted animal

7. HEWT = 7. WHET
   Sharpen

8. ERLADR = 8. LARDER
   Place, such as a pantry or cellar, where food is stored

9. AENB = 9. BANE
   Cause of harm, ruin, or death

10. ECRLPAS = 10. PARCELS
    Packages; wrapped-up items

11. UTTLONGY = 11. GLUTTONY
    Excess in eating or drinking

12. RMINEV = 12. VERMIN
    Pests; people considered hateful or highly offensive

13. ESTAGMRAT = 13. STRATAGEM
    Military plan designed to deceive or surprise an enemy

14. DLSGEE = 14. SLEDGE
    Vehicle mounted on runners, drawn by work animals across ice

15. GINERSG = 15. SNIGGER
    A disrespectful laugh

16. SALPSIOD = 16. DISPOSAL
    To allow one to use or be of service to another

The Lion, The Witch & The Wardrobe Vocabulary Juggle Letters 4

1. EIHTL = 1. _____
   Gracefully slender; moving and blending with ease

2. AGAPNICM = 2. _____
   Military operation or plan

3. EPSRALC = 3. _____
   Packages; wrapped-up items

4. UECSHTRROEA = 4. _____
   Not to be relied on; not dependable or trustworthy; dangerous

5. YSBALTE = 5. _____
   Very disagreeable; unpleasant

6. LITRFE = 6. _____
   Something of little importance or value

7. YOLMCNLAEH = 7. _____
   Sadness or depression of the spirits

8. AXHO = 8. _____
   An act intended to deceive or trick

9. YSLKU = 9. _____
   Pouting and withdrawn

10. NRECUAT = 10. _____
    Mythical being that is half man and half horse

11. UOOPSDIIGR = 11. _____
    Impressively great in size or force

12. OVIPNIAL = 12. _____
    Ornate tent

13. EDNIOOFGRB = 13. _____
    Sense of impending evil or misfortune

14. UTRRTE = 14. _____
    Small tower extending above a building

15. YRUQRA = 15. _____
    Prey; a hunted animal

16. SOIDSALP = 16. _____
    To allow one to use or be of service to another

The Lion, The Witch & The Wardrobe Vocabulary Juggle Letters 4 Answer Key

1. EIHTL = 1. LITHE
Gracefully slender; moving and blending with ease

2. AGAPNICM = 2. CAMPAIGN
Military operation or plan

3. EPSRALC = 3. PARCELS
Packages; wrapped-up items

4. UECSHTRROEA = 4. TREACHEROUS
Not to be relied on; not dependable or trustworthy; dangerous

5. YSBALTE = 5. BEASTLY
Very disagreeable; unpleasant

6. LITRFE = 6. TRIFLE
Something of little importance or value

7. YOLMCNLAEH = 7. MELANCHOLY
Sadness or depression of the spirits

8. AXHO = 8. HOAX
An act intended to deceive or trick

9. YSLKU = 9. SULKY
Pouting and withdrawn

10. NRECUAT =10. CENTAUR
Mythical being that is half man and half horse

11. UOOPSDIIGR =11. PRODIGIOUS
Impressively great in size or force

12. OVIPNIAL =12. PAVILION
Ornate tent

13. EDNIOOFGRB =13. FOREBODING
Sense of impending evil or misfortune

14. UTRRTE =14. TURRET
Small tower extending above a building

15. YRUQRA =15. QUARRY
Prey; a hunted animal

16. SOIDSALP =16. DISPOSAL
To allow one to use or be of service to another

ABIDE	Put up with; tolerate
ALIGHTING	Coming down and settling, as after flight
ALLIANCE	Political partnership
BANE	Cause of harm, ruin, or death
BEASTLY	Very disagreeable; unpleasant

BECKONED	Signaled or summoned, as by nodding or waving
BOUGHS	Tree branches, especially large or main branches
BRISTLING	Standing stiffly on end
BURRING	A buzzing or whirring sound
CAMPAIGN	Military operation or plan

CAMPHOR	Compound made of bark and leaves, used to repel insects
CENTAUR	Mythical being that is half man and half horse
CORDIAL	Invigorating & stimulating tonic
DECOY	Something used to lure victims into danger
DIN	Loud, harsh noise

DISPOSAL	To allow one to use or be of service to another
DOMINION	Territory of influence or control; realm
DRATTED	Frustrating; cursed
ENCHANTED	Influenced by charms or spells
FESTOONS	Decorative garlands of flowers or leaves

FOREBODING	Sense of impending evil or misfortune
FRATERNIZING	Associating with others in a brotherly way
GAIETY	State of joyful exuberance or merriment
GIBBER	Rapidly speak about unimportant matters
GLADE	Open space in a forest

GLUTTONY	Excess in eating or drinking
HEARTILY	With warmth and sincerity
HOAX	An act intended to deceive or trick
INCANTATION	Words believed to have a magical effect; a spell
INQUISITIVE	Inclined to investigate; eager for knowledge

JEERING	Verbal abuse; taunting
JOLLIFICATION	Festivity; revelry
LABURNUM	Kind of tree with clusters of yellow flowers
LARDER	Place, such as a pantry or cellar, where food is stored
LEERING	Look with a sidelong glance with evil intent

LITHE	Gracefully slender; moving and blending with ease
LULLING	Soothing; calming; causing to sleep or rest
MANTLE	Loose, sleeveless coat worn over outer garments; cloak
MELANCHOLY	Sadness or depression of the spirits
MUFFLER	Heavy scarf worn around the neck for warmth

ORDINARY	Of no exceptional ability
PARCELS	Packages; wrapped-up items
PAVILION	Ornate tent
PEDLARS	British word for one who travels about selling wares
PREMISES	A building and its surrounding grounds

PRODIGIOUS	Impressively great in size or force
PROPHECY	Prediction of the future
QUARRY	Prey; a hunted animal
RABBLE	Disorderly crowd of people
RECKONED	Relied on with confidence

REMNANTS	Left-overs
RENOUNCED	Given up, especially by formal announcement
REPULSIVE	Offensive or disgusting
RESUMED	Began again; continued after interruption
SATYR	Mythological creature composed of part man and part goat

SHORN	Shaved
SHRILL	High-pitched and piercing in tone or sound
SLEDGE	Vehicle mounted on runners, drawn by work animals across ice
SLUICE	Kind of gate that controls the rate of water flow through a channel
SNAPPISHLY	In an irritable and short-tempered manner

SNIGGER	A disrespectful laugh
SOLEMN	Deeply earnest, serious, and sober
SPIRES	Structures that taper to a point at the top
SPITEFUL	Showing ill will and a desire to hurt
SPRINGY	Elastic, soft, bouncy

STAG	The adult male of various deer
STRATAGEM	Military plan designed to deceive or surprise an enemy
SULKY	Pouting and withdrawn
TOKEN	Something serving as proof of something else; a sign
TREACHEROUS	Not to be relied on; not dependable or trustworthy; dangerous

TRIFLE	Something of little importance or value
TROOPED	Moved as a group
TURRET	Small tower extending above a building
VELVET	Cover over with a soft, furry covering
VENTURED	Took a risk; dared

VERMIN	Pests; people considered hateful or highly offensive
WARDROBE	Tall cabinet or closet built to hold clothes
WHET	Sharpen
WRETCHED	Of a poor or mean character

Lion, Witch & Wardrobe Vocab

SLUICE	WHET	LULLING	VERMIN	PEDLARS
SHORN	BURRING	GLADE	RECKONED	GAIETY
FRATERNIZING	DECOY	FREE SPACE	TRIFLE	PAVILION
ORDINARY	HEARTILY	SNIGGER	QUARRY	RESUMED
GIBBER	VELVET	BRISTLING	WRETCHED	LABURNUM

Lion, Witch & Wardrobe Vocab

FOREBODING	MANTLE	BANE	INCANTATION	GLUTTONY
SOLEMN	LEERING	HOAX	SULKY	CAMPHOR
LITHE	PROPHECY	FREE SPACE	FESTOONS	RENOUNCED
ENCHANTED	REPULSIVE	SPITEFUL	PARCELS	SPRINGY
PREMISES	SNAPPISHLY	JEERING	BEASTLY	DOMINION

Lion, Witch & Wardrobe Vocab

SHRILL	JOLLIFICATION	DIN	RESUMED	SPITEFUL
VENTURED	PEDLARS	SNIGGER	LARDER	PAVILION
SHORN	LULLING	FREE SPACE	BEASTLY	ALIGHTING
CENTAUR	WHET	LEERING	RECKONED	ABIDE
WRETCHED	BECKONED	INCANTATION	CORDIAL	QUARRY

Lion, Witch & Wardrobe Vocab

RENOUNCED	BRISTLING	STAG	LABURNUM	TROOPED
VERMIN	JEERING	CAMPHOR	ENCHANTED	FOREBODING
GLADE	TRIFLE	FREE SPACE	PROPHECY	BANE
SULKY	INQUISITIVE	MUFFLER	SPIRES	PARCELS
SLEDGE	RABBLE	GLUTTONY	TURRET	REMNANTS

Lion, Witch & Wardrobe Vocab

FRATERNIZING	DECOY	DOMINION	BRISTLING	RECKONED
LITHE	DIN	ENCHANTED	PAVILION	SHORN
FOREBODING	TOKEN	FREE SPACE	PRODIGIOUS	MANTLE
SLEDGE	QUARRY	REPULSIVE	SLUICE	CAMPHOR
HOAX	WRETCHED	INCANTATION	SNAPPISHLY	VERMIN

Lion, Witch & Wardrobe Vocab

ABIDE	SULKY	GAIETY	SPRINGY	LULLING
STRATAGEM	CENTAUR	REMNANTS	ALLIANCE	RABBLE
WHET	TURRET	FREE SPACE	SPIRES	BURRING
PARCELS	SOLEMN	VELVET	GLADE	BECKONED
PEDLARS	DRATTED	LEERING	LARDER	VENTURED

Lion, Witch & Wardrobe Vocab

BOUGHS	INQUISITIVE	PEDLARS	RABBLE	ALIGHTING
LEERING	ALLIANCE	TRIFLE	WHET	RESUMED
ENCHANTED	SHRILL	FREE SPACE	SULKY	ORDINARY
STAG	ABIDE	LITHE	DOMINION	SPITEFUL
MELANCHOLY	LULLING	VENTURED	CORDIAL	GLUTTONY

Lion, Witch & Wardrobe Vocab

BECKONED	REPULSIVE	PREMISES	VELVET	SPIRES
JOLLIFICATION	SPRINGY	SLEDGE	MANTLE	GIBBER
PRODIGIOUS	CAMPHOR	FREE SPACE	CAMPAIGN	QUARRY
DRATTED	PARCELS	INCANTATION	DIN	SNAPPISHLY
DISPOSAL	SOLEMN	STRATAGEM	HOAX	WRETCHED

Lion, Witch & Wardrobe Vocab

JOLLIFICATION	SPITEFUL	SNIGGER	VELVET	SNAPPISHLY
CAMPAIGN	WARDROBE	TOKEN	BRISTLING	VENTURED
SHORN	TREACHEROUS	FREE SPACE	BOUGHS	PEDLARS
SLEDGE	PAVILION	BANE	JEERING	PRODIGIOUS
INCANTATION	CAMPHOR	ENCHANTED	LARDER	GAIETY

Lion, Witch & Wardrobe Vocab

INQUISITIVE	MANTLE	WHET	RESUMED	STRATAGEM
SPRINGY	SATYR	TRIFLE	FOREBODING	ABIDE
ORDINARY	PARCELS	FREE SPACE	SULKY	STAG
LABURNUM	VERMIN	GIBBER	BEASTLY	ALLIANCE
REPULSIVE	MELANCHOLY	RABBLE	HEARTILY	BURRING

Lion, Witch & Wardrobe Vocab

PROPHECY	FOREBODING	BANE	GLADE	VENTURED
BOUGHS	TOKEN	TREACHEROUS	SATYR	QUARRY
HOAX	SOLEMN	FREE SPACE	TURRET	INCANTATION
SPIRES	GAIETY	VELVET	RECKONED	SHRILL
WARDROBE	LABURNUM	SPRINGY	STRATAGEM	REPULSIVE

Lion, Witch & Wardrobe Vocab

PAVILION	WRETCHED	SHORN	SNIGGER	WHET
GIBBER	HEARTILY	GLUTTONY	SNAPPISHLY	SPITEFUL
BEASTLY	JEERING	FREE SPACE	MELANCHOLY	ALLIANCE
LARDER	TRIFLE	CORDIAL	DECOY	ABIDE
BECKONED	BRISTLING	BURRING	FRATERNIZING	SLEDGE

Lion, Witch & Wardrobe Vocab

STAG	GIBBER	LULLING	SHORN	TROOPED
SLEDGE	SPIRES	PAVILION	BOUGHS	BECKONED
ENCHANTED	PROPHECY	FREE SPACE	QUARRY	TURRET
REPULSIVE	JOLLIFICATION	SPITEFUL	BURRING	DISPOSAL
MELANCHOLY	GAIETY	TREACHEROUS	INQUISITIVE	VELVET

Lion, Witch & Wardrobe Vocab

SNAPPISHLY	TOKEN	PRODIGIOUS	LEERING	WRETCHED
DECOY	LABURNUM	SHRILL	REMNANTS	RENOUNCED
TRIFLE	JEERING	FREE SPACE	SNIGGER	RABBLE
ALIGHTING	PARCELS	ABIDE	HEARTILY	BRISTLING
SULKY	FRATERNIZING	DRATTED	SLUICE	BANE

Lion, Witch & Wardrobe Vocab

PAVILION	MANTLE	CAMPAIGN	PEDLARS	PROPHECY
CAMPHOR	PARCELS	SULKY	JOLLIFICATION	STAG
TROOPED	RESUMED	FREE SPACE	SHORN	BANE
RECKONED	SPITEFUL	MELANCHOLY	VELVET	SOLEMN
ENCHANTED	ALLIANCE	CENTAUR	RABBLE	TRIFLE

Lion, Witch & Wardrobe Vocab

INQUISITIVE	HEARTILY	INCANTATION	GLUTTONY	SLUICE
BRISTLING	LABURNUM	TURRET	ABIDE	REPULSIVE
PREMISES	SNAPPISHLY	FREE SPACE	DECOY	SATYR
SLEDGE	LITHE	FESTOONS	VENTURED	FRATERNIZING
TREACHEROUS	LARDER	BEASTLY	SHRILL	DOMINION

Lion, Witch & Wardrobe Vocab

PAVILION	CORDIAL	ENCHANTED	VELVET	MANTLE
WARDROBE	FOREBODING	LULLING	GAIETY	FESTOONS
RENOUNCED	WRETCHED	FREE SPACE	SHORN	DOMINION
BURRING	HEARTILY	WHET	INCANTATION	SPIRES
LARDER	TREACHEROUS	STRATAGEM	PARCELS	ALLIANCE

Lion, Witch & Wardrobe Vocab

SNIGGER	CAMPHOR	BANE	GLUTTONY	ABIDE
SOLEMN	TURRET	SLEDGE	HOAX	LEERING
RESUMED	LABURNUM	FREE SPACE	DRATTED	CENTAUR
SLUICE	SHRILL	CAMPAIGN	GLADE	SNAPPISHLY
DECOY	FRATERNIZING	DISPOSAL	SULKY	REPULSIVE

Lion, Witch & Wardrobe Vocab

PREMISES	ALLIANCE	DECOY	DOMINION	BANE
TRIFLE	CAMPHOR	QUARRY	SOLEMN	VERMIN
DISPOSAL	SLUICE	FREE SPACE	INQUISITIVE	REPULSIVE
ORDINARY	REMNANTS	LEERING	BOUGHS	PRODIGIOUS
HOAX	PAVILION	GIBBER	SLEDGE	ENCHANTED

Lion, Witch & Wardrobe Vocab

ALIGHTING	RECKONED	JOLLIFICATION	SATYR	INCANTATION
DRATTED	TURRET	VENTURED	WHET	SNAPPISHLY
MANTLE	FESTOONS	FREE SPACE	FRATERNIZING	CORDIAL
STRATAGEM	WRETCHED	PROPHECY	MUFFLER	RENOUNCED
SHORN	SPRINGY	BEASTLY	BECKONED	MELANCHOLY

Lion, Witch & Wardrobe Vocab

PRODIGIOUS	HEARTILY	CORDIAL	FESTOONS	SNIGGER
RESUMED	TURRET	MUFFLER	ORDINARY	DOMINION
SOLEMN	SATYR	FREE SPACE	RECKONED	BOUGHS
FOREBODING	SLEDGE	SPITEFUL	SULKY	ALLIANCE
INQUISITIVE	RABBLE	FRATERNIZING	WHET	TOKEN

Lion, Witch & Wardrobe Vocab

LITHE	TRIFLE	JEERING	SHORN	PEDLARS
VERMIN	BECKONED	CAMPAIGN	ENCHANTED	QUARRY
MELANCHOLY	CENTAUR	FREE SPACE	DRATTED	INCANTATION
BANE	DECOY	ABIDE	CAMPHOR	ALIGHTING
STAG	TREACHEROUS	BURRING	SHRILL	LEERING

Lion, Witch & Wardrobe Vocab

SPRINGY	RESUMED	RENOUNCED	DOMINION	SHORN
PEDLARS	PROPHECY	GLUTTONY	SHRILL	PRODIGIOUS
ABIDE	DIN	FREE SPACE	STRATAGEM	WHET
SULKY	DISPOSAL	TROOPED	VERMIN	DRATTED
SLUICE	FESTOONS	ORDINARY	TURRET	STAG

Lion, Witch & Wardrobe Vocab

QUARRY	PAVILION	ENCHANTED	GIBBER	BEASTLY
CENTAUR	SLEDGE	REPULSIVE	FOREBODING	SPITEFUL
TOKEN	GLADE	FREE SPACE	BOUGHS	TRIFLE
DECOY	TREACHEROUS	WRETCHED	PREMISES	INQUISITIVE
MANTLE	CORDIAL	JEERING	BANE	LARDER

Lion, Witch & Wardrobe Vocab

BANE	PREMISES	MUFFLER	SNIGGER	CENTAUR
ORDINARY	INQUISITIVE	TOKEN	BOUGHS	TURRET
DOMINION	ALLIANCE	FREE SPACE	CAMPHOR	GIBBER
CAMPAIGN	SLEDGE	SHORN	PARCELS	STAG
LITHE	TRIFLE	BURRING	VENTURED	LABURNUM

Lion, Witch & Wardrobe Vocab

SHRILL	SULKY	DRATTED	ABIDE	PROPHECY
TROOPED	LARDER	VERMIN	SPRINGY	SPIRES
JEERING	SOLEMN	FREE SPACE	GAIETY	RABBLE
BRISTLING	MELANCHOLY	PAVILION	MANTLE	REMNANTS
WHET	DISPOSAL	ALIGHTING	QUARRY	RESUMED

Lion, Witch & Wardrobe Vocab

PREMISES	DIN	LITHE	JEERING	QUARRY
SPRINGY	CAMPAIGN	GLADE	ORDINARY	TOKEN
FESTOONS	SHORN	FREE SPACE	LULLING	LEERING
JOLLIFICATION	DISPOSAL	REPULSIVE	CORDIAL	VERMIN
SOLEMN	GLUTTONY	ENCHANTED	ALLIANCE	PRODIGIOUS

Lion, Witch & Wardrobe Vocab

STRATAGEM	TURRET	DECOY	CENTAUR	HEARTILY
INCANTATION	PAVILION	INQUISITIVE	MANTLE	LABURNUM
TROOPED	BEASTLY	FREE SPACE	PROPHECY	SNIGGER
PARCELS	GAIETY	RESUMED	RABBLE	SHRILL
ABIDE	BECKONED	SATYR	RECKONED	STAG

Lion, Witch & Wardrobe Vocab

LULLING	SOLEMN	WHET	WRETCHED	ALLIANCE
LABURNUM	BANE	SNIGGER	LARDER	PAVILION
TRIFLE	ORDINARY	FREE SPACE	GIBBER	INCANTATION
JEERING	PARCELS	GAIETY	QUARRY	FOREBODING
REMNANTS	BEASTLY	MANTLE	SATYR	MUFFLER

Lion, Witch & Wardrobe Vocab

CENTAUR	SHRILL	BOUGHS	CORDIAL	ENCHANTED
SPITEFUL	CAMPAIGN	ABIDE	DECOY	LITHE
TROOPED	SULKY	FREE SPACE	LEERING	JOLLIFICATION
RECKONED	DISPOSAL	PREMISES	PROPHECY	TURRET
MELANCHOLY	ALIGHTING	DOMINION	SLEDGE	SPIRES

Lion, Witch & Wardrobe Vocab

FOREBODING	SNIGGER	TRIFLE	WRETCHED	SLUICE
HOAX	CAMPAIGN	JOLLIFICATION	RABBLE	TOKEN
BANE	HEARTILY	FREE SPACE	DECOY	VELVET
SATYR	TREACHEROUS	PARCELS	MELANCHOLY	DISPOSAL
SNAPPISHLY	STRATAGEM	SLEDGE	ALIGHTING	REMNANTS

Lion, Witch & Wardrobe Vocab

MANTLE	TURRET	GLADE	BOUGHS	BEASTLY
ORDINARY	DIN	SHRILL	WHET	BECKONED
CENTAUR	SPITEFUL	FREE SPACE	STAG	INCANTATION
RESUMED	RECKONED	FRATERNIZING	FESTOONS	SHORN
GLUTTONY	TROOPED	CAMPHOR	WARDROBE	GIBBER

www.ingramcontent.com/pod-product-compliance
Lightning Source LLC
Chambersburg PA
CBHW081452070526
44586CB00019B/2316